Beakers in Britain and Europe: Four Studies

Contributions to a Symposium
organised by the
Munro Lectureship Committee,
Edinburgh University

edited by
Roger Mercer

Contributors:

Lawrence Barfield, Humphrey Case,
Richard Harrison and Stephen Shennan

BAR Supplementary Series 26
1977

British Archaeological Reports

122, Banbury Road, Oxford OX2 7BP, England

GENERAL EDITORS

A. C. C. Brodribb, M.A. A. R. Hands, B.Sc., M.A., D.Phil.
Mrs. Y. M. Hands D. R. Walker, M.A.

B.A.R. Supplementary Series, 26, 1977: "Beakers in Britain and Europe: Four Studies"

© The individual authors, 1977

The authors' moral rights under the 1988 UK Copyright, Designs and Patents Act are hereby expressly asserted.

All rights reserved. No part of this work may be copied, reproduced, stored, sold, distributed, scanned, saved in any form of digital format or transmitted in any form digitally, without the written permission of the Publisher.

ISBN 9780904531831 paperback
ISBN 9781407343136 e-book
DOI https://doi.org/10.30861/9780904531831
A catalogue record for this book is available from the British Library
This book is available at www.barpublishing.com

CONTENTS

	Page
INTRODUCTION	1
1. THE BELL BEAKER CULTURES OF WESTERN AND SOUTH WESTERN EUROPE R. J. Harrison	5
2. THE BEAKER CULTURE IN ITALY L. H. Barfield	27
3. THE APPEARANCE OF THE BELL BEAKER ASSEMBLAGE IN CENTRAL EUROPE S. J. Shennan	51
4. THE BEAKER CULTURE IN BRITAIN AND IRELAND H. J. Case	71

LIST OF CONTRIBUTORS

R. J. Harrison,
Department of Classics,
University of Bristol.

L. H. Barfield,
Department of Ancient History and Archaeology,
University of Birmingham.

S. J. Shennan,
Department of Archaeology,
University of Southampton.

H. J. Case,
Ashmolean Museum,
Oxford.

EDITOR

R. J. Mercer,
Department of Archaeology,
University of Edinburgh.

LIST OF FIGURES

Figure		Page
1: 1	Distribution of All Over Corded Beakers in Western Europe	21
1: 2	Distribution of Comb decorated Maritime Beakers (heringbone variety) in Western Europe	22
1: 3	Distribution of Cord zoned Maritime Beakers in Western Europe	23
1: 4	Schematic Representation of the VNSP - Maritime Beaker continuity model	24
1: 5	Distribution of VNSP II and Maritime beaker sites around the Tagus estuary, Portugal	25
1: 6	Distribution of the Later Beaker Cultures in the Iberian Peninsula	26
2: 1	Distribution and location map of Beaker sites in Italy	37
2: 2	'Begleitkeramik' from Monte Covolo	38
2: 3	'Begleitkeramik' from Sant' Ilario	39
2: 4	Modes of zone decoration on Italian beakers	40
2: 5	Beakers from Monte Covolo	41
2: 6	Beakers from Monte Covolo	42
2: 7	Beaker motifs from Monte Covolo	43
2: 8	Beakers from Sant' Ilario	44
2: 9	Beaker motifs from Sant' Ilario	45
2:10	Beaker motifs from the Veneto and Lombardy	46
2:11	Beaker motifs from Emilia	47
2:12	Beakers from Tanaccia di Brisighella	48
2:13	Beaker and 'Begleitkeramik' from Tanaccia di Brisighella and Borgo Panigale	49
3: 1	Examples of Bell Beakers from Bohemia	63
3: 2	Examples of Bell Beaker accompanying pottery from Bohemia	64
3: 3	Bar graph of number of graves and types of goods in graves in Bohemiam Corded Ware and Bell Beakers	65

Figure		Page
3: 4	Distribution of Bell Beaker sites in Bohemia and Moravia in relation to soil types	67
3: 5	Distribution of Bell Beaker sites in Bohemia and Moravia in relation to soil types	69
3: 6	Chronological Interrelationships of the Late Neolithic - EBA in the major Bell Beaker areas of Central Europe	70
4: 1	Provisional dispersion diagrams of radiocarbon dates for British beakers, urns and food-vessels and some Northwest European beaker groups	90
4: 2	Provisional dispersion diagrams of radiocarbon dates	92
4: 3	Early style beakers from Cassington, Oxon. and grave groups with Middle style beakers from southern England	94
4: 4	Middle style beakers and grave groups from Northern England	96
4: 5	Diagram plans of Cassington and Eynsham cemeteries and diagram of orientation of skeletons in these two cemeteries	98
4: 6	Grave groups with Late style beakers	100

BEAKER STUDIES IN BRITAIN AND EUROPE

INTRODUCTION

The existence of a European ceramic style - one readily identifiable and relatively homegeneous - known by the appellation 'Beaker' or 'Bell Beaker' pottery has been recognised since the later years of the nineteenth century. Montelius (1898), Abercromby (1912) and Reinecke (1902) among others all recognised the widespread affinities of this pottery style and also perceived the regular association of the pottery with a consistent group of other non-ceramic artefacts. That some of these artefacts were of cuprous metal placed the development fairly clearly during the opening phases of the formal Bronze Age, although most early workers were hesitant (e.g. Abercromby) about the degree to which the style evolved during the Latest Neolithic period. In Britain and in NW Europe the work of Bryce, Rutimeyer and, later, other physical anthropologists added a further dimension to this complex. The pottery and its associated artefacts were normally found in inhumation graves and many, although by no means all, of the crania studied from these graves were markedly different in form, strikingly brachycephalic, than those of earlier populations. It was a natural step, within Britain at any rate, for Abercromby to speak of 'invaders' bringing the pots, or the technique of making them, to these islands. In Europe as a whole in the late twenties and early thirties, several regional studies of Beakers appeared (Neumann 1929, Bursch 1933) and in 1927 an overall review of the European evidence was attempted by Castillo (1927). The superficially very striking similarity in pottery style over very widely dispersed areas seemed to furnish a much needed horizon of uniformity at a crucial stage of European prehistory when horizontal "dowels" for locking together the various vertical chronological schemes composed largely on regional typology were notably scarce. With the benefit of hind-sight it would seem likely that the desire for one horizon of immediacy led to the over-emphasis of ceramic parallels at the expense of due consideration of the very wide regional variability in the recurrent non-ceramic assemblage. Castillo's work also made the natural advance from the postulation of Pan-European typological and chronological equity to that of invasive diffusion of the ceramic by ethnic groups whose existence was defined solely by the Pan-European ceramic type. He saw the origin of this diffusion lying in Iberia. Thus the terms 'Beaker people' and 'Beaker folk' became much used from the late twenties onwards particularly in Britain where the osteological evidence served to lay emphasis on the differential ethnic content of the period. The insularity of Britain and even the 'socio-psychological' conditions in that country described by Clarke (1966) also served to weight the scales in favour of incursion.

Childe writing in 1929 (Childe 1929) examined the Bell Beakers largely known from inhumation graves in Moravia, Bohemia, Bavaria, Thuringia and on the Middle Danube and in Silesia. The uniformity of the pottery was again a dominant feature for him and he somewhat hesitantly, perhaps, accepted the Iberian origin for the introduction of the pottery style into Central Europe propounded by Castillo. At the same time Childe briefly explored, and discarded as probably too flimsy, the existence of parallels both for Beaker pottery and for associated non-ceramic artefacts in 'Late Danubian' (Vucedol) contexts. Bosch-Gimpera, Leeds and others had already expressed doubts, chiefly based upon the non-uniformity of the skeletal evidence throughout Europe, on the unitary Iberian origin proposed by Castillo. Childe in accepting a unitary diffusion linked it with the diffusion of metal-using, referring to Beaker people as merchants and traders seeking metal resources and dispensing metal products.

By 1930 the lines had been drawn therefore which were to dominate all consideration of Beaker pottery and its association for the next thirty years until the 1960's. The two major initial contributions in this latter period of study are probably those of Piggott (1963) and Sangmeister (1963) and both sought to expand the basis upon which Beaker Studies had hitherto been conducted. Both examined on an equal footing the ceramic evidence and the evidence of non-ceramic associations in an attempt to define for the first time a Beaker culture or a series of Beaker Cultures in the true Childean sense of "a recurrent assemblage of artefacts". Sangmeister attempted to cover the whole of Europe and in the absence of a secure chronological footing produced a splendid rationalisation of the essentially contradictory evidence in which he saw on the basis of ceramic and non-ceramic typology, and with the aid of the earlier findings and conclusions of the Stuttgart metal analysis programme, two fundamental movements within Europe diffusing what has become known since as the "Beaker package" - firstly a movement out of Iberia following Castillo (Castillo 1954) into Central Europe and then a second Rückstrom or 'reflux' movement from Central Europe carrying a rather different assemblage into the Rhineland, the Low Countries and ultimately Britain. It was in Britain specifically that Piggott opened his enquiry. Using Sangmeister's 'reflux' theory as a backcloth Piggott recognised, partly in response to the first radiocarbon dates coming in for beaker graves in the early sixties, the extended chronology of the Beaker occupation of this country. He recognised two early relatively small scale incursions followed by a series of insular developments - concepts with which perhaps few scholars would now disagree fundamentally. His approach was however based, in so far as the ceramic evidence was concerned, upon the corpus of pottery compiled by Abercromby in 1912 and at about the same time he was writing the late David Clarke was commencing the vital groundwork of a complete corpus of Beaker pottery in Britain. The first modern corpus of beakers in Europe was perhaps that of Van der Waals and Glasbergen (1955) and their emphasis on zonal decoration and its analysis was followed by Clarke. His computer matrix analysis of the pottery on the basis of decorative motif and form led to the construction of a complex sequence of invasion events drawing upon continental parallels for their putative origins. The chronology of these events was founded upon the available uncalibrated radiocarbon dates and again emphasised and expanded the considerable span of time over which Beaker innovation was occurring. Cognate with, and succeeding upon these incursions a long and complex series of insular developments were postulated. The emphasis which Clarke's scheme placed upon purely ceramic considerations together with the other great catalyst leading to present developments in thought - the increase in the number and range of radiocarbon dates available for beaker associations - has led to criticism of his British scheme particularly by Dutch colleagues working on similar material and examining the immediate continental forbears of his incursive sequence (Lanting and Van de Waals 1972) and, by virtue of the increased availability of radiocarbon dates, placing more and more emphasis on the importance of Northern corded ware forms in the initial development of the Beaker tradition. Yet Clarke's work still stands as a monument in the development of British Beaker studies and the acknowledged sound foundations of subsequent work.

With the calibration of radiocarbon dates into calendar years after the work of Suess upon the Californian Bristlecone Pine Dendrochronological sequence the span of Beaker activity has been expanded over even wider chronological limits. A paper (HJC) within this symposium shows British Beaker development as now extending well over the span of a millenium.

With the loss of the immediacy of Castillo's, and even to some extent Sangmeister's, view of Beaker development the concept of ethnic invasion has become, to some, less attractive. Both Clarke himself (Clarke 1976) and Burgess and Shennan (1976) have pointed to the degree to which within Britain at any rate a number of hitherto accepted "invasive" features of the so-called "Beaker package" can be traced within long-standing native tradition. It will be seen that the relationship between the Pan-European Beaker tradition and the many native Neolithic groups with which it came into contact is one of the 'leitmotivs' of the papers composing this symposium.

It was the intended function of the symposium held in Edinburgh in February 1976 to place various aspects of recent British research into the European Beaker phenomenon in context with one another before a large audience of lay, undergraduate and graduate composition. The publication of these papers will, it is hoped, place before a far wider audience a brief statement of the state of present research, comprehensible to the lay audience and accompanied by up to date and full bibliographies adequate for most undergraduate and post graduate purposes. It is to be hoped that this can be achieved at a price which will place this information readily within the reach of that wider audience to which we have referred.

The editor must finally place on record his thanks to the Munro Committee of the University of Edinburgh and its convener David Ridgway without whose enthusiasm the symposium could not have taken place, and his warm gratitude to the four contributors for their promptitude and patience. Robert Munro himself, it is hoped, would have been pleased by the European scope and yet high British relevance of the content of the symposium and the desire to inform as wide an audience as possible of results of up to date thinking and research. He may also have felt some gratification that the names of his good friend Lord John Abercromby and successive holders of the Abercromby chair of Archaeology within Edinburgh University, Vere Gordon Childe and Stuart Piggott should figure so largely in the history of research in this peculiarly difficult but vital area of European prehistory.

BIBLIOGRAPHY

Abercromby J. (1912), A study of the Bronze Age pottery in Great Britain and Ireland and its associated Grave Goods, Vol. I.

Burgess C., and Shennan S., 'The Beaker phenomenon: some suggestions' in Settlement and Economy in the Third and Second Millenium B.C. eds. Burgess C., and Miket R., (1976), 309.

Bursch F. C., (1933), Oudheidkundige Mededeelingen van het Rijksmuseum van Oudheden te Leiden N.S. XIV, 39-123.

Castillo A. del Yurrifa (1928), La Cultura del Vaso Campaniforme.

Castillo A. del Yurrifa (1954), El Vaso Campaniforme cordado en la Peninsula Iberica Cronica del IV Congreso Internacional de Ciencias Prehistoricas y Protohistoricas, 445-58.

Childe V. G., (1929), The Danube in Prehistory.

Clarke J. G. D. (1966), 'The Invasion hypothesis in British Archaeology', Antiquity, XL, 172-189.

Clarke D. L., (1970), Beaker Pottery of Great Britain and Ireland

Clarke D. L., (1976), 'The Beaker network - social and economic models', Glockenbecher Symposion Oberried 1974.

Lanting J. N. and Van der Waals J. D. (1972), 'British Beakers as seen from the Continent' Helenium XII, 20-46.

Montelius O. (1898), 'Chronologie der älteste Bronzezeit in Norden Deutschlands und Skandinavien' Archiv für Anthropologie XXV, 443-483.

Neumann E. (1929), 'Die Gleiderung der Glockenbecker in Mittel Deutshlands Prahistorische Zeitschrift XX

Piggott S. (1963), 'Abercromby and after: the Beaker cultures of Britain re-examined' Culture and Environment: Essays in honour of Sir Cyril Fox ed. Foster I. and Alcock A. L., 53-91.

Reinecke P. (1902), 'Beiträge zur kentnis der früheren Bronzezeit Mitteleuropas' Mitteilungen der Anthropologische Gesellschaft in Wien XXXII, 104-129.

Sangmeister E. (1963), 'La Civilisation du Vase Campaniforme' Actes du premier Colloque Atlantique, Brest 1961.

Sangmeister E. (1967), 'Die Datierung des Rückstroms der Glockenbecher und ihre Answirkung auf die Chronologie der Kupferzeit im Portugal' Palaeohistoria XII, 395.

1. BEAKER CULTURES OF IBERIA, FRANCE AND THE WEST MEDITERRANEAN ISLANDS, 2200-1500 B.C.

Richard J. Harrison

INTRODUCTION

It is over 45 years since Childe (1930:201) was able to write "... It would be eminently satisfactory if a convincing pedigree for the bell-beaker cultures could be worked out in detail, with the aid of the abundant material available; a material so rich as to leave few gaps that must be filled by hypothesis." Despite the passage of time and the accumulation of information, the same gaps that Childe remarked upon survive. This essay is designed to provide some hypotheses to span the tantalizing lacunae and suggest some fresh approaches based on newly discovered (or in some cases, rediscovered) regularities now apparent in the French and Iberian Beaker cultures. The three chief points to consider are, firstly, the sort of information that is actually available, and the most fruitful methodology to apply to it. Secondly, the case for the origin of the earliest Beakers in the Iberian Peninsula needs careful consideration, since not only must it be plausible in regional terms, but it must also harmonize with the substantial evidence from France (Guilane, 1967; Treinen, 1970) and the West Mediterranean in general (Bray, 1964; Contu, 1966; Peretti, 1966). Lastly, the development of the later and highly distinctive Beaker cultures in Iberia and Southern France requires discussion.

I. MATERIALS AND METHODS

Unlike North West and Central Europe, the Peninsula and France have relatively few closed Beaker finds, and an even smaller number of satisfactorily stratified deposits. There are probably less than 50 reliable grave lots and stratified assemblages from the whole area under consideration, and with the exception of Provence, C14 dates are all too rare. However, there are certain positive features in both Iberia and France which are notably lacking in other areas of dense Beaker occupation.

In Iberia there is an abundance of rich settlements of all kinds; large and small open sites, large fortified citadels, seasonal occupations in economically marginal territories etc. In addition, a wide variety of caves, rock shelters and megalithic tombs have provided an enormous amount of material. Indeed, densities in Central Portugal and South West France are among the highest in Europe. Despite this richness it is hard to control the samples with rigour, since they are so severely distorted by irrational factors, such as the proximity of a great modern city, an assiduous local worker, or the preferential survival of sturdy monuments, such as megalithic tombs. But for all these caveats, the situation is more promising than that in North West and Central Europe, where studies are based almost exclusively on burials, and upon the typology of one pot form; the Bell Beaker. The domestic and settlement data so scarce in other regions will form a significant part of this paper.

The other choice body of material especially well represented is metal; ores, tools, weapons, crucibles and furnaces. The possession of a complete metallurgical technology is an important aspect of the Bell Beaker cultures, and any consideration about the rise and spread of Beakers must satisfactorily account for this technical ability. A demonstration of ceramic "continuity" is insufficient by itself (Lanting et al. 1973). Metallurgy is manifestly not a sudden development but a complex technology with a long ancestry.

Features that are so familiar among the Beaker cultures elsewhere in Europe are almost absent from Iberia and France; there are extra-ordinarily few tumuli over any Beaker burials, and cremations and flat cemeteries can be numbered in single figures.

In such circumstances it is sensible to rely upon the distribution of types, modes and traits in order to isolate discrete patterns and association frequencies from "mixed" assemblages. Some areas are necessarily much better researched than others, among them Central and Northern Portugal, North East Spain, Languedoc and Brittany. There, distributions can be relied upon whereas the "concentrations" around Madrid, for example, merely reflect the proximity of the modern capital. If equally intense interference with the landscape had occurred elsewhere on the Meseta, it is likely that similar densities would appear. Distributions and association frequencies can be cross-checked against the closed finds and stratified assemblages in order to avoid the grosser sorts of systemic error. Finally, the whole edifice rests upon careful typological method, not the fiddling around with one pot form and a few hundred grave lots, but using all the information on hand. The Type Variety System (TVS) (Smith, Willey and Gifford, 1960; Sabloff and Smith, 1969) developed in the USA is particularly well suited for isolating recurring trait clusters, and ranking them. The beauty of the system is that types can be defined by separate criteria for each type, and so long as they work for the systematizer, they are valid. What is essential is the recognition that types and typologies must be constructed for very specific purposes, and that no single typology is likely to accommodate all the demands placed upon it. The types in this essay are defined according to the TVS, and retained because they function well.

A useful general approach is the culture basin (kulturkreis) theory developed by Graebner (1905) and Wissler (1917), since neither Iberia nor France are cultural units. They are more like South Eastern Europe with a very distinctive set of stable culture-areas that have strong environmental and geographic constraints. Within these areas, such as Almería, Central Portugal or Brittany, it makes sense to treat Beakers as a culture like other cultures (and therefore susceptible to similar analysis and comparison), and to consider them in relation to long-established regional patterns ("Culture-History Trajectories"). Such a model dispenses with the need for such agents of hectic culture change as "warriors", "nomads", "traders", "missionaries" and the like (Childe, 1958), a farrago which even in their own terms are hardly capable of demonstration, let alone proof. Recent theories of "peddlars" (Sangmeister, 1972), using 17-19th century examples from North America seem equally unhelpful, and are methodologically invalid, resting upon a selection of ethnographic parallels to create a specific analogy. The models of systemic and processual culture change developed in the USA on the basis of exceptionally rich and well documented case studies cannot yet be used, since the rigorous controls required[1] are still lacking.

THE EARLIEST BEAKERS; ORIGIN AND CONTINUITY

Neither in the Peninsula nor in France is there any <u>direct</u> stratigraphical evidence to establish the priority of the oldest Beaker style, but reference to the clearer and better dated sequence in Holland (Lanting et al. 1973) strongly suggests that the All Over Corded Beaker (AOC) is earlier than the Maritime type (M), with thin bands of herringbone decoration executed with a comb (e.g., Alapraia; Leisner, 1965). The AOC and M types are especially important since they are the most widespread and recognisable forms, and were already established by 2000 bc on C14 evidence.

The AOC Beakers (Fig. 1.1) concentrate in the Rhineland, Eastern Britain and Brittany, with a scatter in Languedoc and Eastern France. They are very rare in Spain, and wholly absent in Portugal and Southern Spain. Only one site in Iberia has a significant number of AOC sherds (Filomena, Castellón de la Plana), and they are clearly intrusive into the Peninsula, making little impact there (Castillo, 1954). Despite evidence for the longevity of AOC styles in Eastern and Northern Britain, they appear to be a short-lived type in the rest of Europe, disappearing around 1800 bc.

The M Beaker distribution is quite distinct (Fig. 1.2), contrasting very clearly with the AOC pattern. There is a massive coastal concentration in the South and West, especially in Brittany, Languedoc, and above all, Central Portugal, where they occur <u>en masse.</u> Maritime Beakers are also the <u>only</u> early form known in Sardinia, Sicily, Morocco and Southern Spain.

Intermediate between the AOC and M distribution is the pattern of the Cord-Zoned Maritime Beaker (CZM) (Fig. 1.3), which is an early Hybrid form between the AOC and M types. This distribution tends to confirm that both the AOC and M forms have separate backgrounds which may well be the results of quite distinct lines of ceramic development. Also noticeable is that the Maritime Beaker is the only early type represented in <u>every</u> region in France as well as the Iberian Peninsula. Radiocarbon dates (GrN) of 2100 ± 40 bc for Maritime Beakers at Zambujal in Central Portugal,[2] allied to the dates of 2000-1900 bc from Holland and the distinct distribution pattern are the chief reasons for accepting an early date for the Maritime Beaker.[3] The only regions where all three early types (AOC, M, CZM) occur in roughly proportional quantities are Brittany and Languedoc. Intriguingly, in Brittany there are hardly any later Beaker forms at all, and nothing that can be recognised as a late Beaker culture such as develops elsewhere in Southern France, Britain or Iberia.

The significance of these three distributions is supported by a detailed look at the Maritime distribution in Central Portugal. The argument for the local development of the Maritime Beaker from a Vila Nova de São Pedro (VNSP) background has already been outlined (Harrison, 1974, 1974a), but it is worth setting out in a little more detail (Fig. 1:4).

The early phases of the VNSP culture are obscure, but it is recognisable by 2800 bc, and must be seen as a parallel phenomenon to Los Millares in Almería, flourishing around the same time in the latter half of the third millennium bc. The distinctly fabourable environment of Central Portugal, where the Mediterranean and Atlantic flora intermingle, supported by rich and well-watered soils, is one reason for the great density of large sites in and around the Lisbon peninsula and the Tagus estuary. The argument for interpreting the Maritime Beaker as a local development representing a change in the style of luxury decorated ceramic rests on a variety of mutually reinforcing patterns discernable in settlements, burials, technology and trade patterns.

In the Lisbon and Setúbal peninsulas some dozens of VNSP settlements are known, ranging in size from small hamlets, such as Negrais (Cunha Serrão and Prescott Vicente, 1954) to great fortified citadels girt with bastioned walls and massive rock cut ditches, as at Vila Nova de São Pedro (Jalhay and do Paço, 1945), and Zambujal (Sangmeister and Schubart, 1972). In nearly every single case, excavation and surface collections have shown VNSP II and Maritime Beaker materials in the same levels, and stratigraphic work at the large defended sites of Rotura (Tavares da Silva, 1971), Penha Verde (Zybszewski and Veiga Ferreira, 1958; 1959) have proved beyond reasonable doubt that Maritime Beakers were in use and being locally made in quantity as the preferred form of luxury pottery. Furthermore every settlement site with Maritime Beaker sherds possesses VNSP II material (Fig. 1:5) contrasting nicely with over forty single-period Beaker sites of the Palmela Type, (which is demonstrably a late, local Tagus estuary Beaker culture). The identity of the VNSP-M Beaker settlement pattern is also reflected in the equally emphatic link in burial practice, and its sharp separation from customs followed in the later Palmela Beaker culture.

In particular, the large dry-stone corbel-vaulted tombs[4] which were built in VNSP times to receive interments at regular intervals, have rich Maritime Beaker deposits. The contruction techniques at tombs such as Praia das Maçãs (Leisner et al. 1969) or Pai Mogo I (Spindler and Gallay, 1972) is identical to that observed on the fortified settlements, down to the construction of false cupolas and deep entrances with prominent door jambs. Rock cut tombs, which are largely contemporary with the corbel-vaulted ones, posed no great construction problem either, since huge silos and rock cut ditches are well known from Vila Nova de São Pedro and Zambujal. The same practice of repeated, single inhumations in a collective sepulchre continue, the only difference being that the later burials are accompanied by a new luxury ceramic, the Maritime Beaker. Such rich tombs as São Pedro do Estoril I, Alapraia and Praia des Maçãs (Leisner, 1965) show that repeated Maritime Beaker interments were the rule. Even more interestingly, there is not one known case in the whole of Central Portugal of either a VNSP or a Maritime Beaker single burial. This well studied region has not produced either, and probably never will, since it is unlikely that such single burials were ever made. Burials of later Palmela Beaker types do not, with one exception,[5] occur _en masse_ in the great collective tombs, but are very common in the simpler "dolmens", rock shelters and caves, such as the Ponte de Laje, Oeiras (Zbyszewski et al. 1957).

There is a 95% correlation between VNSP and Maritime Beaker settlements and burials, based on a complete study of every site of this period in Central Portugal. In the South and North of Portugal, where VNSP materials are conspicuously absent, Maritime Beakers are rare. Indeed, in Southern Portugal, where hundreds of megalithic tombs were emptied by Heleno in the '30s and '40s, Beakers of any sort are exceedingly rare; less than four sites are known, and all are of the Palmela complex. There is therefore a very strong case for interpreting the Maritime Beaker as part of the VNSP cultural assemblage, and not as an intrusive phenomenon from elsewhere.

Metalworking technology illustrates the same points. The evidence for Iberia has recently been summarized (Harrison, 1974a), where by plotting trace element patterns published by JSS[6] on logarithmic graphs, clear groups were defined. The same trace element pattern in most graphs is noticeable, and the increasingly strong preference for an arsenical copper culminates with this alloy being deliberately chosen for certain types of implement. Early phases of VNSP metallurgy were characterized by an erratic use of arsenical copper and numerous tools made from pure copper. Although awls, small flat axes, and chisels occur in both VNSP and Maritime Beaker levels of the major settlements, only certain classes of object have high arsenic contents, such as the Palmela Points, a distinctive Beaker artefact. Other types, such as the axes, were mainly of pure copper, or only rarely of arsenical copper. True tin bronze was known in only a very few cases, and was not in general use in Central Portugal until the Atlantic EBA c.1500 B.C. Among other improvements in Beaker metallurgy was the widespread use of polishing and cold hammering to improve the surface finish and hardness, but such characteristically Beaker techniques were rare in VNSP times, and are normally only found on a small number of flat axes.

An entire metal-working furnace of Beaker date has been discovered at Zambujal, securely stratified below a large hollow stone tower which itself contained Beaker sherds in its upper fill.[7] The furnace was set in a circular stone walled enclosure containing a large clay doughnut ("Lehmring"), surrounded by ash-filled hearths, one of which held a Maritime Beaker sherd. Inside the lehmring was a thick layer of sharp, clean sand, used as a matrix for casting, and containing large amounts of copper droplets, waste fragments of copper, pieces of awls and small flat axes. Along one wall of the enclosure was a low bench, and the furnace was located in such a manner that fuel could have been stored in a large space at its rear. From an occupation layer in the house, contemporary with the use of the furnace, many plain crucible fragments, VNSP II decorated sherds, Maritime Bell Beakers, flint arrowheads, knives and blades, polished stone axes and copper fragments were found. Crucible fragments are known from other VNSP settlements, including Rotura, Vila Nova de São Pedro, Pedra do Ouro and Penha Verde, indicating that the hearth and furnace arrangement at Zambujal was not an isolated occurrence. Copper ore was found at Vila

Nova de São Pedro, where over 13 kg of malachite and azurite suggested a a southern Portugese origin. Further afield, decorated crucibles in Maritime Beaker assemblages occur at El Acebuchal, near Seville, and Cerro de la Virgen, in Granada.[8]

Gold is well known from secure Maritime Beaker contexts, and includes the gold basket earring from Ermegeira, small spiral rings from São Pedro do Estoril I, and little perforated plaques from Palmela (Leisner, 1965). It is usually said to be unknown until the Beaker period, but a gold bead has recently been found in a stratified pre-Beaker level at Zambjal, and a typologically pre-Beaker gold nail-headed pin of VNSP type was excavated at Penha Verde. Gold working is therefore unlikely to be a newly introduced skill, but one already known from VNSP times.

Additional weight for the hypothesis of essential cultural continuity between the VNSP and Maritime complexes is furnished by the stability and longevity of other resource procurement networks. Among the clearest examples are the finds of ivory and callaïs. Ivory was unobtainable in the Iberian Peninsula and the nearest source lay in North West Africa on the steppes of the Maghreb. Ivory is known in pre-Beaker times in Central Portugal and in Southern Spain, and continued in use into the Beaker period and beyond. Ivory V-perforated buttons are known from Palmela, El Acebuchal, etc., and ivory remained a valued commodity well into the Argaric Bronze Age. At two Moroccan sites in particular, Maritime Beakers of Central Portuguese type were found in sealed levels, and formed assemblages that were identical to those so densely scattered around the Tagus estuary. Gar Cahal and Caf-Taht-el-Gar (Tarradell, 1955; 1957-8) contain over 90% of the known Beakers in Morocco. There seems to be a clear case of reciprocity here, with ivory being introduced into Iberia as a luxury material, and fine decorated ceramics (i.e., Beaker pottery) being sent to Morocco in exchange. Both Gar Cahal and Caf-Taht-el-Gar are coastal sites, but a few later Palmela sherds are also known on inland Maghreb sites and in isolated contexts (Souville, 1965). Interestingly, they too are imports from the same region of Central Portugal as the Maritime sherds, and can be closely matched there (Gilman and Harrison, in lit.)

Callaïs is a much more difficult commodity to trace since its source or sources remain unknown, and several distinct minerals have undoubtedly been confused in the literature. Small blue and green stone amulets and beads were popular in Portugal and in Cataluña from the 4th Millennium onwards, and the stones continued to be prized in VNSP and Beaker times, as the rich grave goods demonstrate. There seems to be less callaïs in Beaker contexts, and there is none at all in the full Bronze Age, after 1500 bc. But as with the case of ivory, it was a desirable commodity, and the mechanism for its procurement remained intact for a long period. It was very much an Atlantic fashion, being exceedingly rare at Los Millares (and in Southern and Eastern Spain generally), and wholly absent from North Africa. It may be possible to relate the distribution of Maritime Beakers in Brittany and Languedoc to the concentration of callaïs in Central Portugal, since there are strong typological affinities between the Maritime assemblages of these groups. Furthermore, callais is known in quantity in both these areas of France, and it has been strongly suggested, although not proved, that geological formations in these regions contain callaïs. Perhaps a mechanism similar to that for the procurement of ivory was in operation, and the present distributions are all that remain of such a trade network. It is also worth noting that in Languedoc there are numbers of another distinctive Portuguese Beaker artefact, the "idol" type of V-perforated button. Languedoc and Central Portugal are the only centres for this unmistakeable form, although it cannot be very closely dated in the Beaker sequence at the moment.

Lastly, the same ceramic technology can be observed in the manufacture of VNSP fine wares and Maritime Bell Beakers. The same quality is maintained, and a fondness for micaceous inclusions and fine washes stretches back to the early VNSP I period (pre-2500 bc), when the "copos" were current (Savory, 1968: Fig. 42a). Although the Bell Beaker is the dominant pot form, outnumbering its associated open and carinated bowls by 4:1, a coherent background for its form, decoration and design motifs can be found in the decorated ceramics in earlier VNSP contexts. There is an increasing trend in the later phases of the VNSP culture towards a higher proportion of decorated pottery, and it can be shown from stratified levels that Maritime Beaker motifs, zoned decoration and comb stamping are all quite common (Tavares da Silva, 1971; Leisner and Schubart, 1966). The motifs themselves could all be derived from textile designs, woven on upright looms for which there is abundant evidence in the form of decorated loomweights (some of which are comb decorated). Experiments[9] have shown that every Beaker motif in Portugal can be easily woven on a simple loom using either wool or flax, with only one colour for contrast.

To summarize this section, it seems there is enough evidence for an unusually close connection between the VNSP and Maritime Beaker complexes to consider them as one culture, and to provisionally accept a Portuguese origin for the Maritime Bell Beaker. Such Beakers can be seen as the luxury decorated ceramic of the last phase of the VNSP culture; phase III to continue the accepted phasing. No such connection can be shown anywhere else in either Iberia or France, and certainly not at Los Millares where Beakers are very rare indeed, despite their fame. The case Clarke (1970) makes for a Beaker origin in Languedoc fails to satisfy any of the criteria used for the VNSP-M continuity model. The later Beaker groups in both Iberia and France present a wholly different aspect from the Maritime complex.

III THE LATER BEAKER CULTURES

The later Beaker cultures are readily separable from the early AOC, M and CZM types, and with their very distinctive regional distributions they make a marked contrast with the earlier ones. They are really bowl cultures, since open and carinated bowls form the great majority of the luxury decorated ceramics, and Bell Beakers comprise little more than 20-25% of the assemblage (Harrison et al. 1975). The distinct regionalization is reflected in localized preferences for certain fine pottery types, coarse wares and small objects such as buttons. Common to all these cultures are the typological changes observed elsewhere in Beaker pottery, with the decoration contracting into two or three broad zones, and a new and wider range of associations. The association pattern for Iberia and France includes several new features of broadly Central European affinity which make their appearance for the first time. None of these groups have the metallurgical richness of the Maritime complex, nor do they seem to have such a wide and extensive range of luxury or élite commodities. Even the flintwork becomes noticeably poorer, and bifacial arrowheads, knives and daggers become scarce. More positively, all these cultures are characterized by domestic assemblages that are as distinct in their coarse wares as in their finer components, and nearly all come from single period open sites, allowing them to be unequivocally distinguished from the Maritime Beakers. The main groups in Iberia (Fig. 1:6) are the Ciempozuelos, Palmela, Carmona and Salamó ones, and in Languedoc-Provence two more are to be found. There are no comparable late Beaker cultures in Brittany, Eastern France or the Rhône valley, where strong EBA cultures were well established by 1700-1800 bc.

The best known of these groups is the Ciempozuelos culture, occupying the central Spanish Mesetas and acting as a focus for the other three later Beaker cultures at its periphery; Palmela in Central Portugal, Carmona in the Guadalquivir basin in Andalucia; and Salamó in Cataluña, concentrating around Reus and Tarragona. Central European contacts are clearest in a few of the richer single grave burials which are so characgeristic of this complex, and they can, with some adjustment, be linked typologically with items in Southern Germany and Northern Italy. Such forms include a pair of gold button covers, a bone dagger pommel of Polada type (Pago de la Peña Zamora), (Maluquer de Motes, 1960; Martín Valls and Delibes de Castro, 1974), large tanged daggers, stone wristguards and possibly such general and unspecific ideas as V-perforated buttons. Unconvincing attempts have been made to link the fine pottery from Ciempozuelos with the Schönfeldergruppe in Saxo-Thuringia (Behrens, 1969), but it can be equally well suggested to be a Spanish development. The luxury fine ware is nearly always dark and lustrous, sometimes with a chalk paste rubbed on the exterior to enhance the decoration, and distinguished by a band of decoration inside the rim and zoned patterns on the exterior. Sharply carinated profiles predominate. The coarser domestic pottery from such sites as Somaén (Castillo, 1928; 1953) and Almazán (Gamer and Ortego y Frías, 1969) includes large storage vessels with small mouths decorated with coarsely incised geometric patterns. There is a large and important plain ware component, largely unstudied, which also includes high quality bowls and Beakers, some of which are undoubtedly plain Bell Beakers. From Cerro de la Virgen (Schüle and Pellicer, 1966. Vogel and Waterbolk, 1972), radiocarbon dates show the Ciempozuelos complex was already well developed by 1900 bc, and probably overlapped with the Maritime forms. This date is in general agreement with that for the Reinecke A1-2 phases in Southern Germany with which the other elements can be synchronised.

At present the only faunal study available is that from Cerro de la Virgen (Von den Driesch, 1972), showing that cattle and pig were the main domesticates, raised for meat. Sheep/goats were also important and became more so with time, since the environment was gradually deforested and plant cover was reduced to its present meagre state. Much has been made of the small sample of domestic horse bones from the Beaker level, but claims for horse-riding (Schüle 1967) must be firmly rejected, since there is no means of determining whether the horses in question were ridden, eaten or used for draught purposes.[10] Other domesticates included rabbits, which like all the other animals at the site had an unusually light build in response to the arid environment.

The Palmela culture in Portugal occupied the old Maritime Beaker territory and is richly represented on such single-period sites as Montes Claros, Moinha da Fonte do Sol, Alto das Perdizes, etc. as well as numerous rich burials in caves (Veiga Ferreira, 1966). All this marks a break with previous VNSP-Maritime traditions. Although there is a marked decline in the range and quantity of luxury commodities used, the pottery is often clearly derived from Maritime forms. The hammer-rimmed Palmela bowl (see; Leisner, 1965) and squat, open Bell Beakers with incised decoration are nearly always in good, reddish fabrics, associated with a coarse ware assemblage of large storage vessels, plain wares and carinated bowls.

To the south in the Guadalquivir basin, the Carmona culture is most strikingly represented at El Acébuchal (Harrison et al. 1976), a large settlement of several successive occupations excavated by the Englishman, George Bonsor, at the end of the last century. It is clear that several import horizons can be identified, such as the Maritime, then Ciempozuelos and Palmela, out of which an astonishingly baroque culture arose, incorporating the widest variety of vessels of any Beaker culture. These include pedestalled bowls, burnished bowls, lids, stands and several giant carinated forms (Frothingham, 1953). As with the other groups, a rich and varied coarse ware was an integral component. Approximate dates of 1700-1200 B.C. may be reasonable, although C14 dates are lacking.

In Cataluña the Salamó culture can be closely defined, and is clearly derived from the Ciempozuelos pottery styles. It is largely known from cave deposits, used for both burial and habitation, and includes dark, well-made bowls, huge "bomb-shaped pots", and a few rare Bell Beakers (Vilaseca, 1941). The distinctive, square V-bored buttons from the 3 closed graves at Sant Oleguer (Serrà i Rafols, 1950) confirm its very late date since such buttons are common in full Early Bronze Age contexts from 1500 bc onwards. Across the border in Languedoc, the same button pattern is copied in limestone (Durfort Type), and is also of EBA date.

Linked to Cataluña is the Languedocian-Provençal Beaker complex (Guilaine, 1967; Courtin, 1974), which includes the settlement dug by the Taffanels (1957) at Embusco. The finer ceramics are largely bowls, often decorated in an imitation chip-carving technique which is known farther up the Rhône valley, and often thought to be of South German origin.

Recent discoveries of Beaker cist burials at Le Petit Chasseur, Sion, (Geneva) revealed a concentration of truly Central European Beaker materials at the most westerly limit of its distribution, with virtually every piece closely matched to pieces known further East in larger numbers. (Gallay and Spindler, 1972). It includes bow pendants, tanged flint arrowheads, round V-perforated buttons, silver earrings, two-holed wristguards and excised Beakers, all pointing to a Bohemian or South German origin. The whole aspect of the material emphasises the importance of the Rhône valley as a corridor for the penetration of Central European Beaker elements to the Mediterranean. Also in Eastern France, a closed grave at Niederhergheim (Haut-Rhin) produced a polypod bowl, three other vessels (2 with handles) and a Rhenish Bell Beaker (Treinen, 1970 Fig: 26; Sangmeister, 1966). A few polypod bowls are known in Languedoc, and a couple in Sardinia (Bray, 1964), where they can be shown at the tomb of Santi Pedru to be older than Polada materials (Contu, 1966). Such polypod bowls are absent from Spain and Portugal.[11] Such graves as these in Eastern France give a reasonable idea of the route by which the scattered Central European elements could have spread into Languedoc thence to Iberia.

Finally, it is worth noting that one Beaker "type-artefact" which is supposed to throw some light on the vexed question of origins, the wristguard, is almost wholly Early Bronze Age in date and context. Sangmeister's catalogue (1964) shows clearly that the vast majority of wristguards in the Peninsula are Argaric in date, and they are only really common in South East Spain, c. 1800-1500 bc.

CONCLUSION

The one really clear point to emerge from this brief excursus is that definition and discussion of culture-complexes is only profitable on the basis of settlement assemblages, as W. W. Taylor realized 25 years ago (1948). Grave goods and seriations are fascinating in themselves, but their value is limited, and their interrogation has become increasingly less profitable in proportion to their isolation from a settlement pattern.

NOTES

1. Especially chronology, sample size and sample variability.

2. To be published shortly.

3. Noticeably rare in Britain.

4. Still incorrectly called "Tholoi".

5. Palmela itself!

6. Junghans, Sangmeister and Schröder, 1968.

7. Unpublished information included through the courtesy of Dr. Hermanfrid Schubart and Professor Edward Sangmeister.

8. Both unpublished.

9. Unpublished, undertaken for RJH in 1974.

10. No horse riding equipment is known anywhere in the Iberian Peninsula before the Late Bronze Age.

11. Fragments of footed bowls are known from Beniprí (Valencia) and Salamó, but are entirely distinct.

BIBLIOGRAPHY

Behrens, H., 1969, Westliche Einflüss bzw. der Glockenbecherkultur bei den Becherkulturen der DDR. in: <u>Die Neolithischen Becherkulturen im Gebeit der DDR und ihre europäischen Beziehungen,</u> Ed. H. Behrens and F. Schlette, 143-154.

Bray, W., 1964, Sardinian Beakers. <u>P.P.S.</u> XXX, 75-99.

Castillo, A. del, 1928, <u>La Cultura del Vaso Campaniforme; Su Orígen y Extensión en Europa</u> (Barcelona).

Castillo, A. del, 1953, Las tres capas de la Cueva de la Mora de Somaén (Soria). <u>Archivo de Prehistoria Levantina</u> IV, 135-150 (Valencia).

Castillo, A. del, 1954, El vaso campaniforme cordado en la Península Ibérica. <u>International Congress of Prehistoric and Protohistoric Sciences, Madrid,</u> 1954 (Actas..., Zaragoza, 1956, 445-458).

Clarke, D. L., 1970, <u>Beaker Pottery of Great Britain and Ireland.</u> (Cambridge).

Childe, V. G., 1930, The origin of the Bell Beaker. <u>Man</u> XXX, No. 141-2; 200-201.

Childe, V. G., 1958, <u>The Prehistory of European Society</u> (London).

Contu, E., 1966, La tomba dei vasi tetrapodi in località Santi Pedru (Alghero-Sassari) <u>Monumenti Antichi dei Lincei</u> XLVII, 1-202.

Courtin, J., 1974, Le Néolithique de la Provence. <u>Mém. de la Soc. Préhist. Française,</u> t.11.

Cunha Serrão, E. da and E. Prescott Vicente, 1954, Note préliminaire sur la station eneolithique de Negrais. <u>International Congress of Prehistoric and Protohistoric Sciences, Madrid,</u> 1954 (Actas.., Zaragoza, 1956, 601-614).

Frothingham, A. W., 1953, <u>Prehistoric Pottery.</u> The Hispanic Society of America, New York.

Gallay, G., and K. Spindler, 1972, Le Petit-Chasseur - Chronologische und Kulturelle Probleme. <u>Helvetia Archaeologia</u> 10/11.3, 62-89.

Gamer, G., and T. Ortego y Frias, 1969, Neue Beobachtungen am Römischen Lager bei Almazán (Prov. Soria). <u>Madrider Mitteilungen</u> X, 172-184.

Gilman, A., and R. J. Harrison (in press) Trade in the second and third millennia B.C. between the Maghreb and Iberia (<u>Hencken Festchrift</u>).

Graebner, F., 1905, Kulturkreise und Kulturschichten in Ozeanien. <u>Zeit. f. Etnol.</u> XXXVII, 28-53 (Berlin).

Guilaine, J., 1967, La Civilisation du Vase Campaniforme dans les Pyrénées Françaises. (Carcassonne)

Harrison, R. J., 1974, Origins of the Bell Beaker cultures: Some speculations. Antiquity XLVIII, 99-109.

Harrison, R. J., 1974a, A Reconsideration of the Iberian Background to Beaker Metallurgy. Palaeohistoria XVI, 63-105.

Harrison, R. J.; S. Quero and Ma. Carmen Priego, 1975, Beaker Metallurgy in Spain. Antiquity XLIX, 273-278.

Harrison, R. J., T. Bubner and V. Hibbs, 1976, A Catalogue of Bell Beaker Pottery from El Acébuchal (Prov. Sevilla). Madrider Mitt. XVII, 79-141.

Jalhay, E. and A. Do Paço, 1945, El Castro de Vilanova de San Pedro. Actes y Memórias de la Sociedad Española de Antropología, Etnografía y Prehistoria, XX, 5-91.

Junghans, S., E. Sangmeister and M. Schröder, 1968, Ausbreitung der frühesten Metallurgie in Europe während der Kupfer -und Frübronzezeit (Stuttgart).

Lanting, J. N, W. G. Mook, and J. D. Van der Waals, 1973, C14 Chronology and the Beaker problem. Helinium XIII, 38-58.

Leisner, V., 1965, Die Megalithgräber der iberischen Halbinsel: Der Westen. Madrider Forschungen I, 3. (Berlin).

Leisner, V., H. Schubart, 1966, Die Kupferzeitliche Befestigung von Pedra do Ouro/Portugal. Madrider Mitteilungen VII, 9-60.

Leisner, V., G. Zbyszewski and O. da Veiga Ferreira, 1969, Les monuments préhistoriques de Praia das Maças et de Casainhos. Mém. de les Serv. Geol. de Portugal No. 16, (Lisbon).

Maluquer de Motes, J., 1960, Nuevos Hallazgos de la cultura del vaso campaniforme en la Meseta. Zephyrus XI, 119-130.

Martín Valls, R. and G. Delibes de Castro, 1974, (pub. 1975) La Cultura del Vaso Campaniforme en las Campiñas Meridionales del Duero. (El Enterramiento de Fuente-Olmedo, Valladolid). Monografías del Museo Arqueológico de Valladolid, vol. I, (Valladolid). 59pp xi. lám.

Peretti, G., 1966, Une sépulture campaniforme en rapport avec l'alignement des menhirs de Palagglu (Sartène-Corse). Congrès Préhist. de France. Compte Rendu le la XVIIIe. session (Ajaccio, 1966) 230-242 (Paris).

Sabloff, J. A. and R. E. Smith, 1969, The importance of both analytic and taxonomic classification in the Type-Variety System. American Antiquity XXXIV, 278-285.

Sangmeister, E., 1964, Die Schmalen "armschutzplatten". Studien aus Alteuropa. Teil I, 93-122 (Tackenberg-Festschrift, ed. K. Narr, Köln-Graz).

Sangmeister, E., 1966, Die Datierung des Ruckstroms der Glockenbecher und ihre Auswirkung auf die Chronologie der Kupferzeit in Portugal. Palaeohistoria XII, 395-407.

Sangmeister E., 1972, Sozial-Ökonomische Aspekte der Glockenbecherkultur. Homo XXIII, 1/2, 188-203.

Sangmeister, E., and H. Schubart, 1972, Zambujal. Antiquity XLVI, 191-197.

Savory, H. N., 1968, Spain and Portugal (London).

Schüle W., 1967 (1969) Glockenbecher und Hauspferd. Archaeologie und Biologie Forschungsberichte 15, 88-93 (Münchner Kolloquium, 1967. Deutsche Forschungsgemeinschaft).

Schüle W., and M. Pellicer, 1966, El Cerro de la Virgen, Orce (Granada) I. Excavaciónes Arqueológicas en España XLVI. (Madrid).

Serra i Ràfols, J. de C, 1950, Sepulturas con vaso campaniforme descubiertas en Sabadell. Arrahona 1/2, 77-92 (Revista del Museo de la Ciudad de Sabadell).

Smith, R. E., G. R. Willey and J. C. Gifford, 1959-1960, The Type-Variety concept as a basis for the analysis of Maya Pottery. American Antiquity XXV, 330-340.

Souville, G., 1965, Influences de la Péninsule Ibérique sur les civilisations post-néolithiques due Maroc. Miscelánea en Homenaje al Abate Henri Breuil (Ed. Ripoll-Perello, II, 409-422).

Spindler, K. and G. Gallay, 1972, Die Tholos von Pai Mogo/Portugal, Madrider Mitteilungen XIII, 38-108.

Taffanel, O. and J. 1957, La station préhistorique d'Embusco. Cahiers Ligures de Préhistoire et d'Archéologie VI, 53-72.

Tavares da Silva, C., 1971, O povoado Pré-histórico da Rotura. Notas sobre á cerâmica. II Congresso Nacional, Coimbra. 175-192 (Coimbra).

Tarradell, M. 1955, Die Ausgrabung von Gar Cahal ("Schwarze Höhle") in Spanisk Marokko. Germania, XXXIII, 13-23.

Tarradell, M., 1957-1958, Caf Taht el Gar, cueva neolítica en la region de Tetuán (Marruecos). Ampurias XIX-XX, 137-159.

Taylor, W. W., 1948, A Study of Archaeology (Menasha).

Treinen, F., 1970, Les poteries campaniformes en France. Gallia Préhistoire t.XIII, 1 and 2, 53-107; 263-324.

Veiga Ferreira, O. da., 1966, La Culture du Vase Campaniforme au Portugal. Mém. de les Serv. Geol. de Portugal, No.12 (Lisbon).

Vilaseca, S., 1941, Más hallazgos prehistóricos en Arbolí (Prov. de Tarragona). Ampurias III, 45-62.

Vogel, J. C., and H. T. Waterbolk, 1972, Gröningen Radiocarbon Dates, X. Radiocarbon 14, 1. 72-110.

Von den Driesch, A., 1972, <u>Studien über frühe Tierknochenfunde von der Iberischen Halbinsel</u>. (Institut f. Palaeoanatomie, Domestikationforschung u. Ges. der Tiermedizin der Univ. München). Deutsches Archaeologisches Institut, Abt. Madrid. (München).

Wissler, C., 1917, <u>The American Indian</u>. (New York).

Zbyszewski, G., A. Viana and O. da Veiga Ferreira, 1957, A gruta préhistórica de Ponte de Laje (Oeiras). <u>Com. dos. Serviços Geológicos de Portugal</u> XXXVIII, 389-400.

Zbyszewski, G., and O. da Veiga Ferreira, 1958, Estação préhistórica da Penha Verde (Sintra). <u>Com. Dos. Serviços Geologicós de Portugal</u>, XXXIX, 37-57.

Zbyszewski, G., and O. da Veiga Ferreira, 1959, Segunda campanha de escavações na Penha Verde (Sintra). <u>I Congresso Nacional, Lisboa</u>. 401-406 (Lisbon).

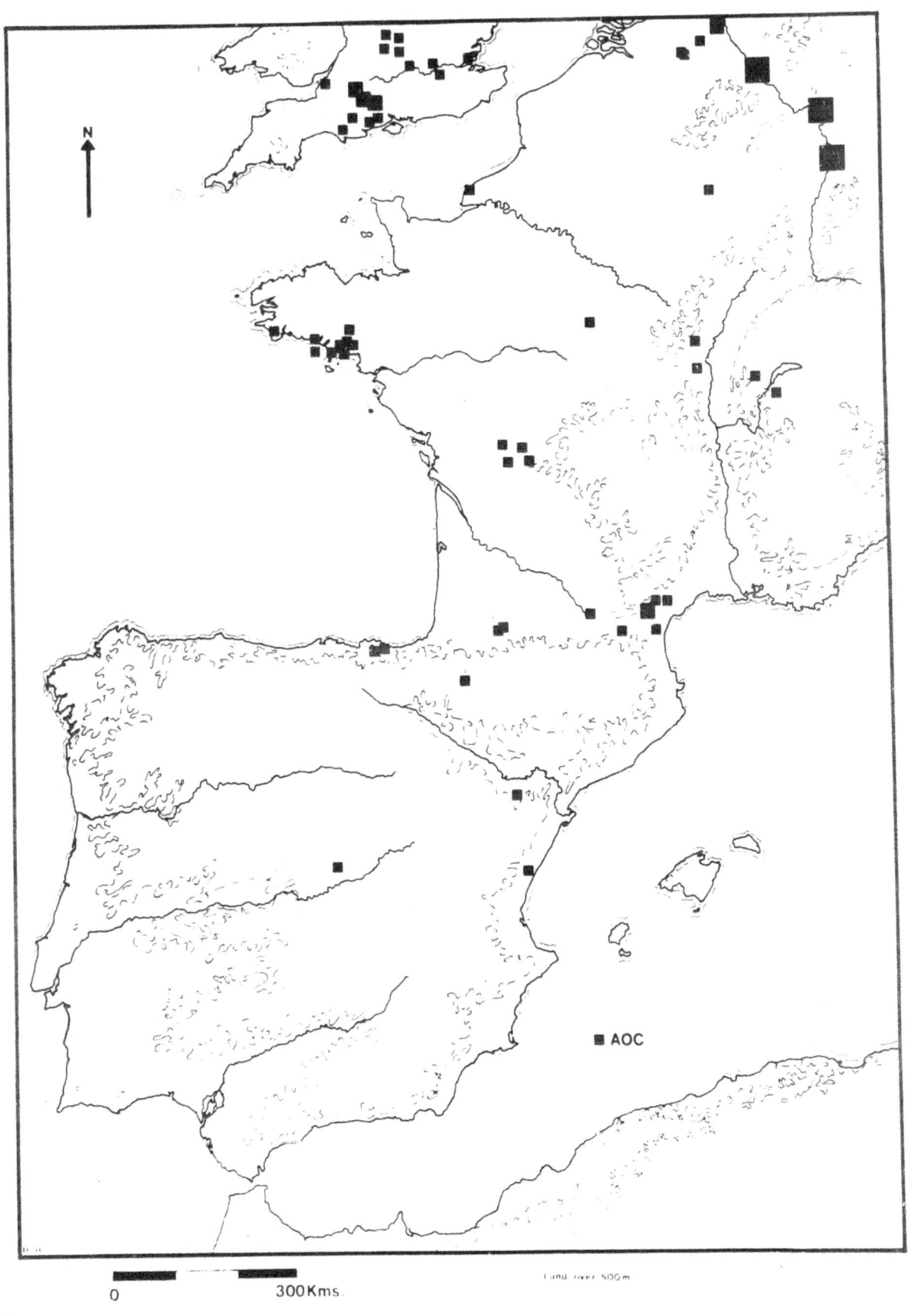

Fig. 1.1   Distribution of All-Over-Corded Beakers in Western Europe.

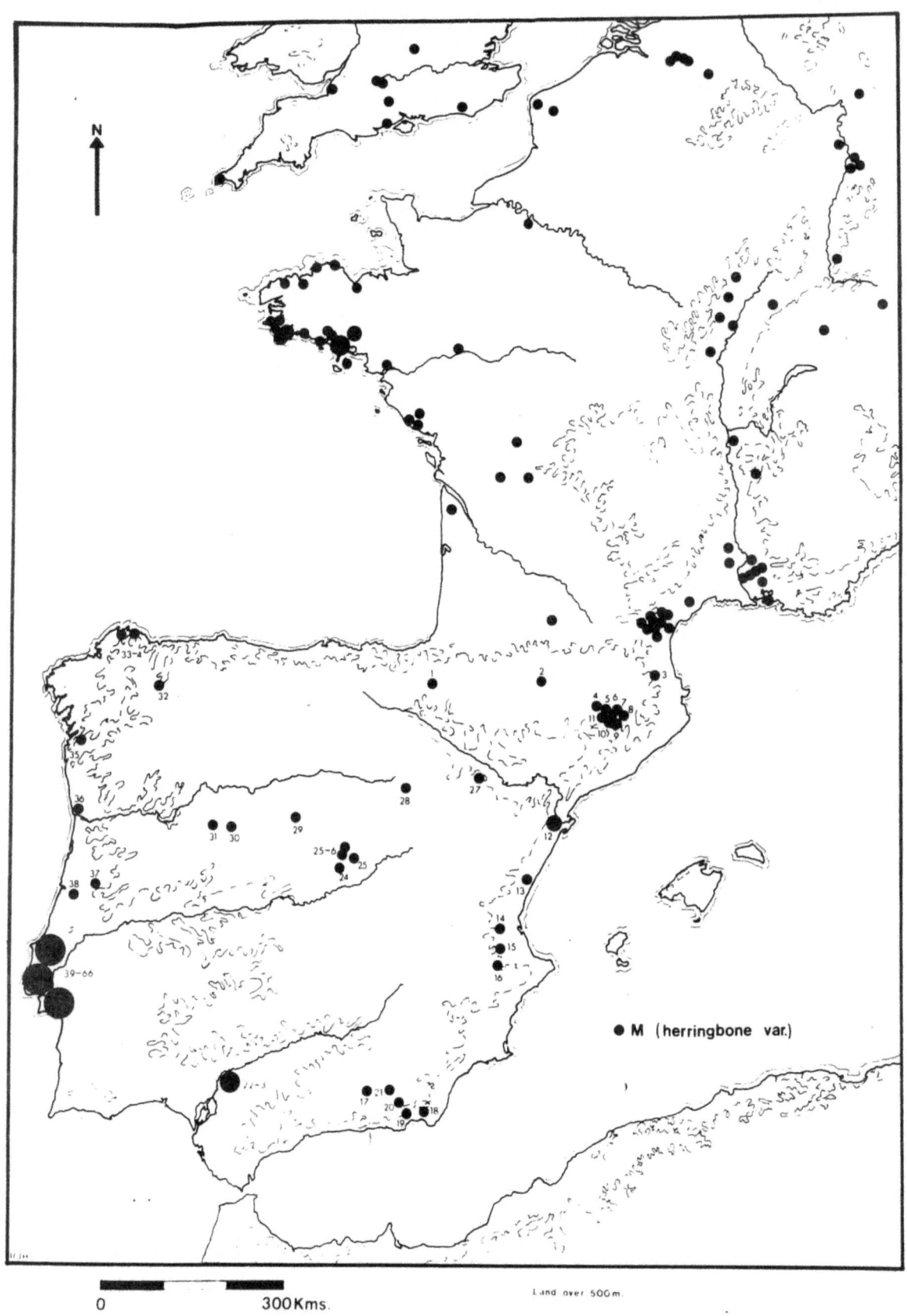

Fig. 1,2   Distribution of comb-decorated Maritime Beakers (Herringbone Variety) in Western Europe.

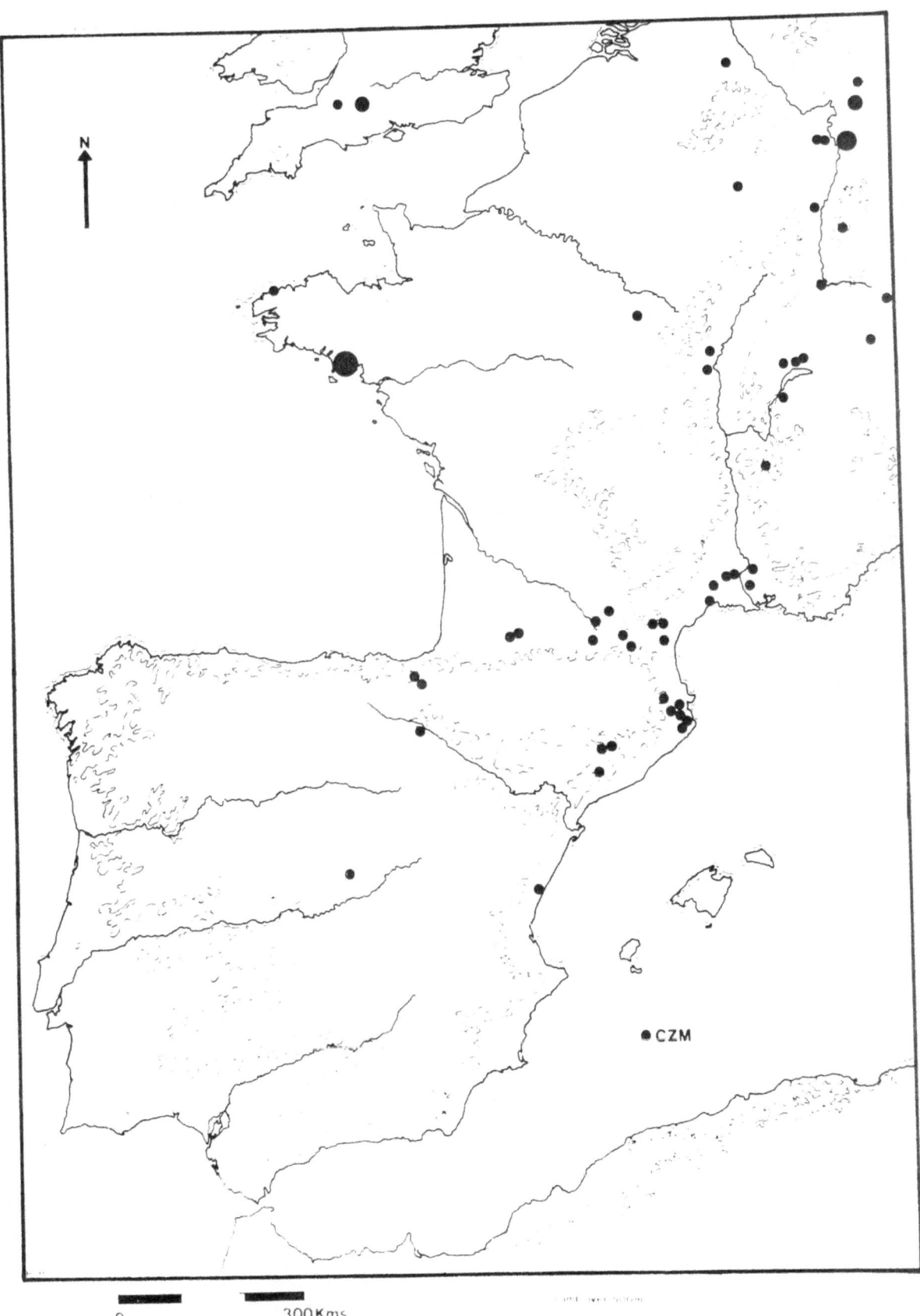

Fig. 3   Distribution of Cord-Zoned Maritime Beakers in Western Europe. (A band of comb decoration is outlined top and bottom by a cord impression, and such bands cover the whole of the vessel).

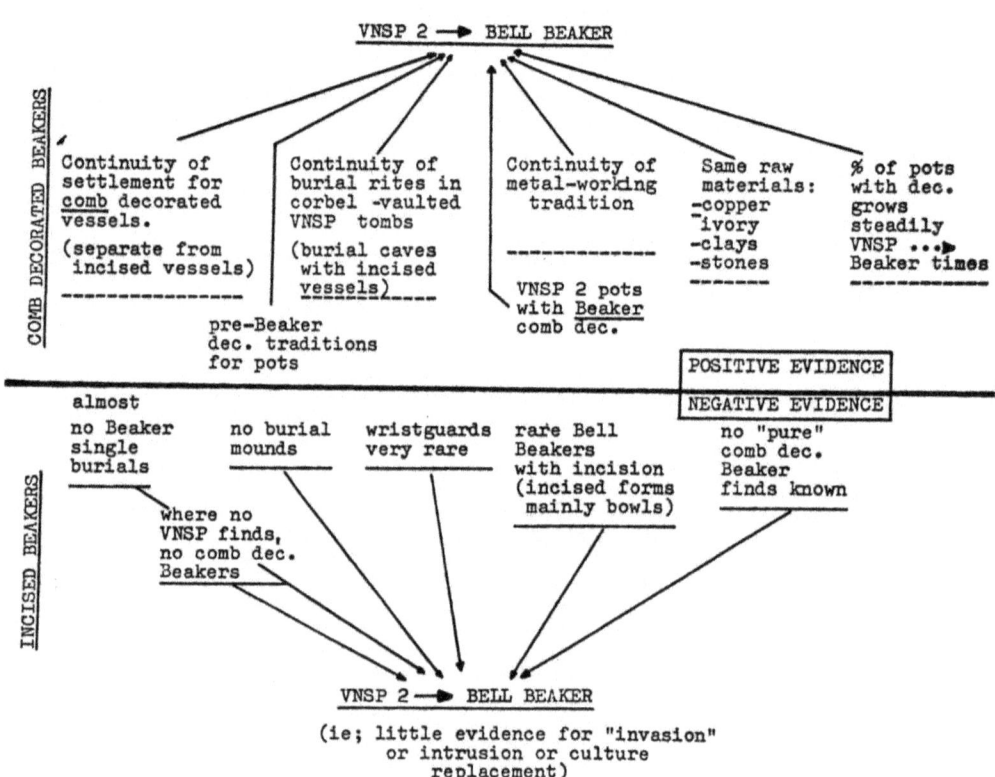

Fig. 1.4 Schematic Representation of the VNSP-Maritime Beaker Continuity Model.

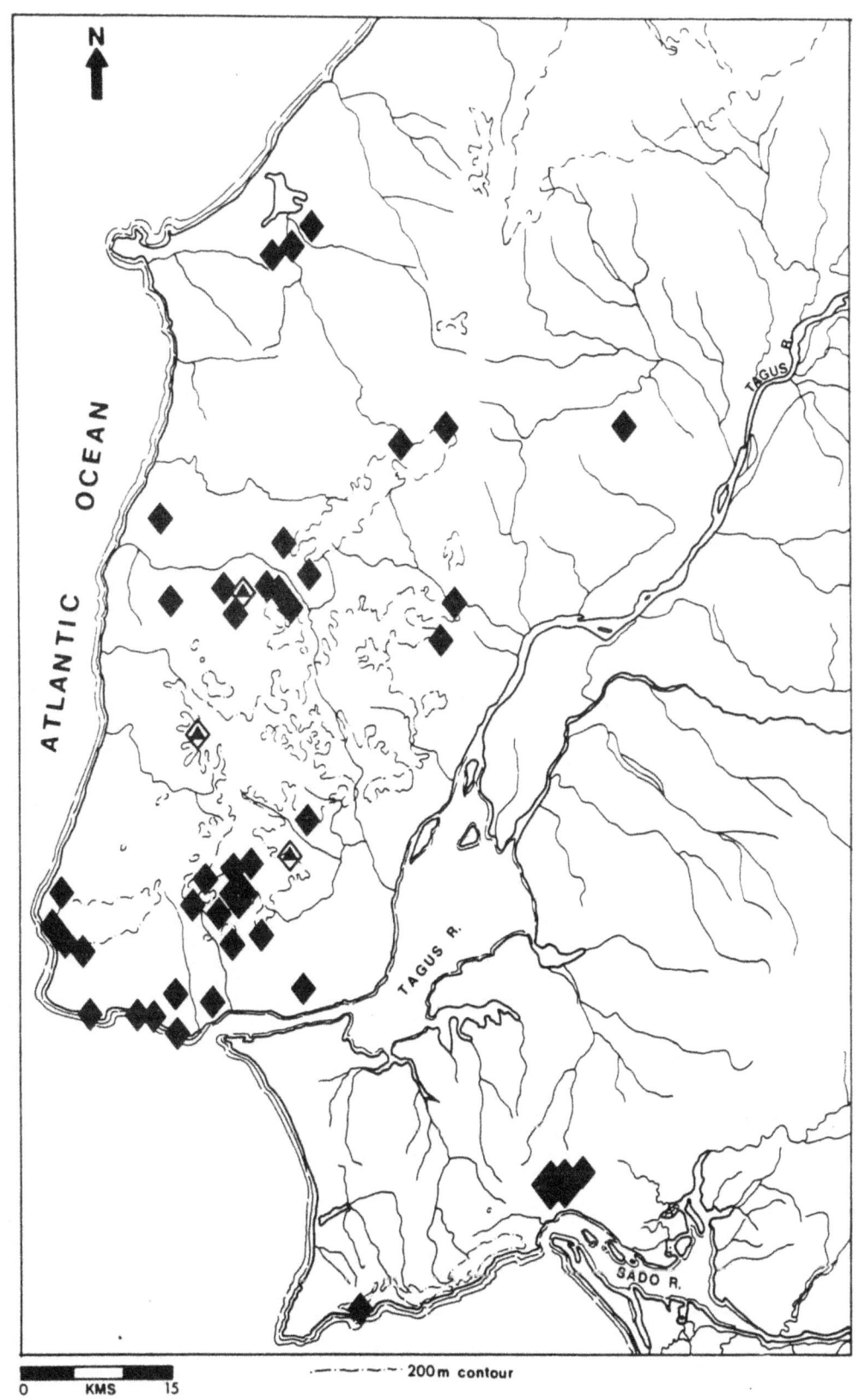

Fig. 1:5   Distribution of VNSP II and Maritime Beaker sites around the Tagus Estuary in Portugal.   Solid symbols indicate that both VNSP II and Maritime Beaker wares occur; hollow symbols show that only VNSP II sherds are present.

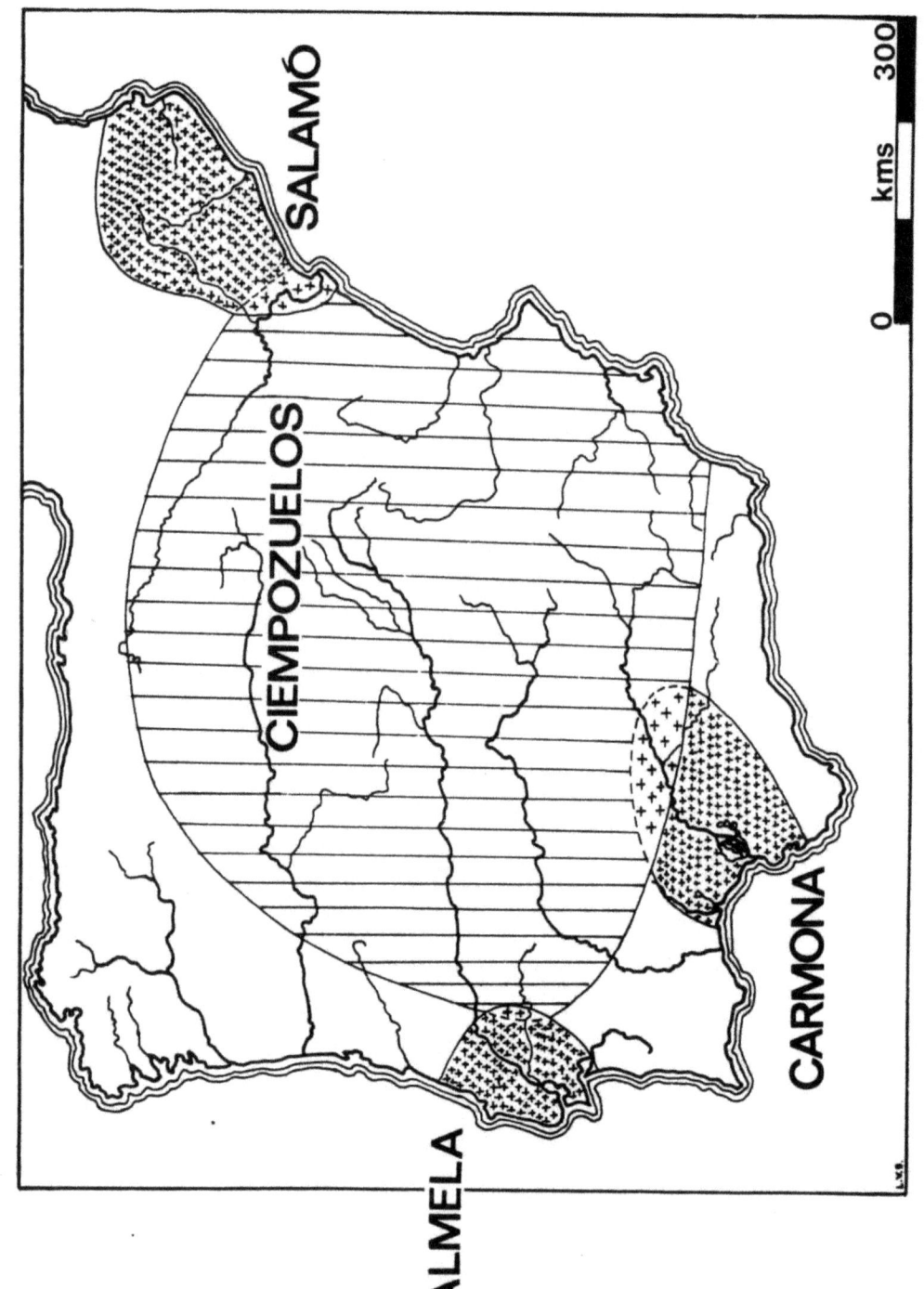

Fig. 1:6 Distribution of the Later Beaker Cultures in the Iberian Peninsula.

2. THE BEAKER CULTURE IN ITALY

L. H. Barfield

INTRODUCTION

How far the material culture of the European Beaker tradition is the product of a single population group with a single source of origin and how far it represents an assemblage acquired by, and integrated with, indigenous Late Neolithic and Copper Age groups remains one of the most controversial questions in the interpretation of the culture. The study of beakers in the Italian peninsula, although offering no easy solution to this problem, at least throws new light on the complexities of the Beaker phenomenon.

DISTRIBUTION OF SITES

The total number of Beaker sites in Italy has increased from six in 1955 (Acanfora 1955) to thirty-nine in 1976 (Fig. 1.).[1]

The beakers come from twenty open settlements, fifteen cave sites and at least five burials.[2]

The open settlements with beakers are mostly hill settlements. In the Pre-Alps and Apennines these are often situated at the point where a valley meets the Po Plain, as at Monte Covolo and Rivoli, on a commanding position dominating a valley route, as at Pescale and Bismantova, or on other naturally fortified positions bordering the Plain, as at Le Colombare and Monte Madarosa in the Monti Lessini and on the Rocca di Manerba and Rocca di Garda on Lake Garda. Some settlements are in the Po Plain itself, like Sant' Ilario on the banks of the Enza and Borgo Panigale near Bologna. The only lake settlements so far to produce beaker finds are Isolino on Varese and a settlement on Lake Monate both in Lombardy.

Cave settlements are characteristic of Liguria and the few settlements from Central and Southern Italy are caves (La Romita di Asciano) or rock shelters (Olevano).

ITALIAN BEAKER ASSOCIATIONS

The majority of these settlements, with the exception of Sant' Ilario and some of the sites in the Monti Lessini, La Sassina, Fanè etc., have produced evidence of a long sequence of prehistoric occupation, with the Late Neolithic and Early Bronze Age periods usually well represented.

This fact, combined with the uncertain stratigraphical position of the beakers on many sites, has meant that it is often difficult to establish the exact cultural context of the Beaker assemblages.

Closely related to this last problem is another, which is how far the beakers on any particular site represent either an integral, indigenous or an intrusive element in the cultural context to which they can be attributed.

On some sites the evidence points to beakers as an alien element in an indigenous cultural tradition. For example, at Le Colombare sherds of two beakers were found in context of a Copper Age settlement related to the Remedello tradition, (Zorzi 1953), and although the stratigraphical position of these beakers is not entirely certain, they are probably contemporary with the Copper Age material. At La Romita di Asciano fragments of a single beaker were found in a Copper Age level, as well in the overlying Early Bronze Age deposits (Peroni 1962-63). On both these sites the rarity of the beaker sherds can perhaps be taken as evidence of their being an intrusive feature on these sites.

At other sites the proportion of beakers to contemporary pottery is much higher. At Sant' Ilario 180 sherds of beaker represent 8.7% of the total sherd count from the site (Barfield et al., 1975) and at Monte Covolo 380 sherds were recovered, of which those from the Beaker levels formed 3.5% of the total sherd count for that horizon (Barfield 1972 and 1973-4). At both sites the similarity between the fabric of the beakers and associated pottery (Begleitkeramik) was also noticed, suggesting a close relationship between the beakers and Begleitkeramik. On these sites, therefore, we can claim that the inhabitants of the settlement themselves were responsible for the production of the beakers found in them.

The beakers from the graves at Santa Cristina (Fig. 2:10, 4-5 and Colini 1899) and Ca di Marco (Fig. 2:10, 1-3 and Colini 1898) appear also to be in a "pure" Beaker culture context to judge from the evidence of mortuary houses at both sites, the tanged copper dagger of Ciempozeulos type at Santa Cristina and short hollow based arrowheads at Ca' di Marco.[3]

The North Italian beakers have, in the past, often been regarded as part of the Remedello culture, (Laviosa Zambotti 1939-40, p 160, Acanfora 1956). This correlation arose due to the close geographical proximity of the graves of Santa Christina and Ca' di Marco to the Remedello cemetery and because of the fact that both produced copper equipment. This view has been held in spite of the fact that the inventory of the Beaker graves differs entirely from that of the approximately 120 burials from Remedello.

A connection between the Beaker assemblages of the north and the Polada culture has for a long time been postulated on account of the similarity of the handled vessel from Ca' di Marco with Polada forms (Laviosa Zambotti 1939-40 p. 159).[4] The Beaker-Polada link has now been further confirmed by new finds of beakers associated with Polada assemblages (Barfield 1975) and also by the recognition of the strong Beaker contribution to the formation of the Polada culture (Barfield 1971, p 78, Aspes and Fasani 1976).

An association of Beaker pottery with Polada material can be demonstrated, albeit with varying degrees of certainty on at least seven sites in the pre-alpine region of the Trentino, Veneto, and Lombardy; Montesei (Trento) (Perini 1972), Praelle di Novaglie (Aspes and Fasani 1974), the Rocca di Rivoli (Barfield 1976b), Fanè and Ca' dei Grii (Biagi and Marchello, 1970) producing the most reliable associations.

The two settlements which have produced the most beakers, however, Monte Covolo and Sant' Ilario, have demonstrated an association of beakers with a range of undecorated pottery which, although clearly related to, and perhaps ancestral to, the Polada tradition, is not strictly to be called Polada.[5] At Monte Covolo the Beaker finds were stratified above a Final Neolithic or Copper Age horizon, which shows affinities with the Swiss Horgen culture, and below a well defined Polada level. The pottery associated with the beakers comprised plain, burnished, 's'-profiled handled cups, amphorae and coarse cooking pots with plain and finger impressed cordons (Fig. 2:2). The handled cups and amphorae show some similarity with the Polada ceramic repertoire, although the use of thickened rims, finger-impressed cordons and the absence of other specific Polada features distinguishes this assemblage from the Polada levels above, and other Polada sites.

The assemblage from Sant' Ilario (Parma) represents a single period of Beaker occupation in which 8.7% of the total sherds are from beakers. The accompanying medium and coarse ware, (Begleitkeramik) (Fig. 2:3), is again certainly not Polada in tradition and has even fewer features in common with Polada than are found at Monte Covolo. The handled bowl with a plug-in handle (Fig. 2:3; 2) is comparable with Polada forms, but the complete absence of Polada style elbow handles is a striking difference. The Sant' Ilario Begleitkeramik also differs noticeably from the Monte Covolo Begleitkeramik in the absence of cordon decoration and the presence of a considerable quantity, 5.1% of total sherds, of finger-nail impressed, coarse ware (Fig. 2:3; 8-11).

To the south of the Polada culture area, Beakers occur with associated pottery and other finds which suggest we are dealing with local variations of an Early Bronze Age cultural tradition, as for example at Tanaccia di Brisighella and Borgo Panigale (Fig. 2:13; 2-3), 5, Scarani 1962, Peroni 1971), La Romita, and Fosso Conicchio.

To summarise, beakers occur in one of three main cultural contexts in Italy.

1) Possibly in Copper Age assemblages;

2) In assemblages which can be regarded as 'pure' Beaker culture which have, however, affinities with the ensuing Polada tradition,

3) In Polada and related Early Bronze Age culture contexts.

BEAKER STYLES AND DECORATION

Since most of the beakers come from settlements and are therefore fragmentary, it is difficult to approach the classification of North Italian Beakers using multiple criteria such as, for example, David Clarke used in classifying the 800 odd complete British Beakers (Clarke 1970).

A useful initial subdivision of the beakers can however be made on basis of the zonal styling. This is a method which both Clarke (Clarke 1970 p 11) and Van der Waals (Van der Waals and Glasbergen 1955) found to be most successful for indicating sub-divisions which had a chronological significance.

In Italy we can provisionally recognise four main zonal styles (Fig.24).

1. All Over Ornament (AOO) with both comb and cord decoration.

2. European, including Pan-European or Maritime.[6]

3. Regular zones combined with one or more broader zones.

4. Very broad bands with a zone or line border.

Whereas styles 1 and 2 are widespread in Europe, styles 3 and 4 would seem to be distinctively Italian. A chronological development from 1 to 4 might be expected and there is some, but unfortunately no conclusive, evidence to back this up.

Of these four zonal styles it is possible that the burials at Ca' di Marco and Santa Cristina, with European beakers, might suggest the existence a pure European or Pan-European phase, although this is by no means certain, since these are from burials and we only have a total of five vessels in this group.

More certainly we can demonstrate that both European and All Over Ornament regularly occur together on sites with beakers of zonal style 3, as at Monte Covolo and Sant' Ilario. At Monte Covolo the bell beaker is the only vessel decorated in Beaker style (Figs. 2:5-7), with a handled version also being represented (Fig. 2:6; 10). Decoration (Fig. 2:5) is mainly executed with comb, but incision, cord impression and even cardium shell impressions (Fig. 2:5; 7) are also found.

The arrangement of the designs is chiefly in zones or All Over Ornament, as well as in zones and lines combined and zones and All Over Ornament combined with broader bands in style 3. Cruciform base decoration is also present (Fig. 2:6; 11, 12). The range of motifs is not very ambitious, with hatched lozenges, reserve zigzags etc. being used in the broader bands on vessels otherwise mainly decorated with obliquely hatched zones. The use of comb impression on fairly large, coarse vessels of uncertain form is a rare occurrence (Fig. 2:6; 9).

The beakers from Sant' Ilario (Figs. 2:8 and 9), while sharing several features of the Monte Covolo range with the same combination of zonal styles, also include significant differences. The main contrasts are to be found in the absence of handled beakers and the presence of beaker bowls (Fig. 2:9; 24-28, 2:8; 9, 10), which are unknown at Monte Covolo, but form a prominent component at Sant' Ilario. The range of decoration, which again is mainly comb with some cord impression, unlike Monte Covolo does not include incision, with the exception of one sherd.

These discrepancies between the Monte Covolo and Sant' Ilario beakers and the more striking differences between their coarse wares, are at present difficult to explain, for to judge from stylistic similarities there would appear to be little chronological difference between the two assemblages, and likewise the geographical distance between the two sites, 90 km, is not great.

Other smaller Beaker assemblages revealed divergences of style of a similar character, although in view of the restricted quantities involved, it would be dangerous to draw conclusions from them at this stage. The Fosso Conicchio beakers, although representing a varied range of design fairly close to the European style, seem, however, to again differ from both the Monte Covolo and the Sant' Ilario beakers. The same can be said for Ca' del Grii, only about 10 km from Monte Covolo, with its curious bulbous beaker shapes and broad band designs below the rim (Fig. 2:10; 28-30).

The Bismantova group (Fig. 11; 8-16) resembles more the Monte Covolo series with its handled beaker, while Pescale (Fig. 11; 17-23) shows a closer connection with the Sant' Ilario series (Malavolti 1942). A further dimension is introduced by the beakers from Montesei (Fig. 2:10; 9-10 and Perini 1972 Fig. 4) and Praelle di Novaglie, which are coarser in quality than those from other sites, and may thus represent a marginal Beaker development.

Other beaker groups and styles must also exist to judge from Kerbschnitt decoration combined with cord impression at Rivoli (Fig. 2:10; 15-17 and Barfield and Bagolini 1976 b Fig. 44) and Kerbschnitt on a new find from near Remedello (Fig. 2:10; 7) (unpublished material), since this technique of decoration does not appear on other sites.

I leave to last perhaps the most coherent, as well as most aberrant, group, which are the beakers from Tanaccia di Brisighella (Fig. 2:11; 1-6 and Figs. 2:12; 2:13, 1-3 and Scarani 1962, Peroni 1971 fig. 37) and Borge Panigale (Fig. 2:13, 4 and 5, Peroni 1971 Fig. 37 [3]) which form a discrete regional style in Romagna.

These are squat vessels, probably all originally with handles (Fig. 2:12; 1, 4), which are decorated with panel designs in the arrangement of zonal style 4. All are decorated with comb. Their direct associations are unclear, although they do seem to be related to plain cups, of a very similar shape to the beakers, and with exaggerated elbow handles, which are found on both the sites in question (Fig. 2:13; 2, 3, 5).

EXTERNAL RELATIONSHIPS OF THE ITALIAN BEAKERS

With regard to the comparison of the Italian Beaker tradition with the Beaker culture elsewhere in Europe we can provisionally note several traits which suggest a connection with a number of different areas of Europe. Cord-outlined zones and All Over Ornament suggest a contact with the South of France or the Rhineland. Handled beakers and the panel designs on beakers from Tanaccia, on the other hand, point to Central Europe, as do the mortuary houses from Ca' di Marco and Santa Cristina, cut-out decoration from Rivoli and the handled, Begleitkeramik bowls from Monte Covolo, Ca' di Marco (Aspes and Fasani 1976) and Sant' Ilario. Finger-nail impressions on coarse ware, as found at Sant' Ilario, remind one of the rusticated coarse pottery in Britain which is associated with several Beaker settlements.[7]

ITALIAN BEAKER CHRONOLOGY

As suggested, the development of the zonal styles might have a chronological significance, as it does in other Beaker areas, and some evidence exists to support this view.

1) The early, Pan-European style is represented in the two possible Copper Age associations at Le Colombare and La Romita.

2) A flat copper axe was found in the Santa Cristina grave with a Pan-European beaker, whereas at both Tanaccia di Brisighella and Borgo Panigale typologically more developed, flanged, copper axes were discovered.

Radiocarbon dates are so far only available from three sites. At Monte Covolo two dates - Birm. 471 2000 ± 320 bc and Birm. 470 1860 ± 210 bc, have too large deviations to be of much use. The dates from two Ligurian sites with beakers, Grotta Pertusello, layer VII, 2440 ± 70 bc (R-155) (Alessio et al. 1967) and Arma di Nasino, level VI, with seven dates ranging from 1370 ± 90 bc (R-259) to 2270 ± 55 bc (R-309) are both unsatisfactory in view of the mixed assemblages associated with the beakers, (Alessio et al. 1968).

CONCLUSIONS

The main conclusions that can be drawn from this study are:-

1. Contrary to what can be shown from Iberia, Holland and Hungary the Italian Beaker tradition is not closely integrated with any local Copper Age cultures but arrives from outside with all its paraphernalia, including coarse pottery. Elbow handles and flint crescents are perhaps among the few native Italian elements to be absorbed.

2. Whereas beakers may be intrusive in the context of the native, Copper Age, Remedello culture they appear to constitute an integral part of the formative stages of the Bronze Age Polada Cultrue.

3. The ancestry of the beakers and their coarse wares suggest a very complex interchange of traits from different parts of the Beaker world, not a single invasion from one direction.

4. The Beaker assemblages are either made up of a single style, i.e. Tannaccia and possibly a pure European phase at Santa Cristina and Ca' di Marco, or more usually of a number of different styles in use at one time.

From this we can see that beakers from settlements are a truer indicator of the stylistic associations of beakers than single beaker finds from graves. The latter, as in the case of Northern Europe, can usually only be grouped typologically.[8] (Note 8: An observation already made by D. L. Clarke [1970, 35]).

5. Beaker decoration in Italy probably evolves through a series of zonal styles although it is as yet difficult to prove this conclusively.

6. That more research and discovery will reveal an even more complex pattern of styles and groups.

FOOTNOTE

The economy of the settlements is not discussed in this article. Monte Covolo and Sant' Ilario have produced both faunal and floral remains of which preliminary results are available (Barfield et al. 1975, Barker 1975).

NOTES

1. In addition, fourteen sites in Sicily have produced beakers, which are not considered in this paper. For recent discussions of the Sicilian beakers see Marconi Bovio 1963 and Barfield 1976A.

2. At the cave site of Ca' dei Grii (Brescia) beakers may be associated with burials (Biagi and Marchello 1970).

3. The burials at Fosso Conicchio show a greater mixture of native and Beaker tradition for the six beakers here, although associated with wristguards, were deposited in a rock-cut tomb of Rinaldone type (Colonna 1970, Peroni 1971, Ridgway 1972).

4. A similar link between Remedello and Polada based on the presence of so-called Polada handles in Remedello further complicates the picture; for this, see (Laviosa Zambotti 1938-40, Barfield and Fasani 1972 and Barfield 1976A).

5. The term Proto-Polada which has been suggested (Aspes and Fasani 1976), needs more precise definition and is not at present a useful concept. We prefer the term Beaker 'Begleitkeramik'.

6. Clarke's term "European" beaker is preferable to the more usual term Pan-European in that it is not so narrowly defined and is thus more suitable for describing the zonal style (Clarke 1970, 18).

7. A fuller discussion of external relationships of the North Italian Beakers will be published with the final report of Monte Covolo.

BIBLIOGRAPHY

Acanfora, M. O. 1956, Fontanella Mantovana e la cultura di Remedello. Bull. Paletn. It. 65, 321-385.

Alessio, M., F. Bella, F. Bachechi and C. Cortesi, 1967, University of Rome Carbon-14 Dates V. Radiocarbon 9, 346-367.

Alessio, M., F. Bella, C. Cortesi, and B. Graziadei, 1968, University of Rome Carbon-14 Dates VI. Radiocarbon 10, 350-364.

Aspes, A. and Fasani, L., 1974, Praelle di Novaglie. Bollettino del Museo Civico di Storia Naturale, I, 527-530.

Aspes, A. and L. Fasani, 1976, Influssi della cultura del vaso campaniforme dell' Europa centrale sulla cultura di Polada. Glockenbecher Symposium, Oberried 1974.

Barfield, L. H., 1971, Northern Italy before Rome, London.

Barfield, L. H., 1972, Scavo di un insediamento neolitico e della prima età del bronzo sul Monte Covolo. Annali del Museo di Gavardo 10, 5-16.

Barfield, L. H., 1973-4, Scavi a Monte Covolo 1973: Seconda nota preliminare. Annali del Museo di Gavardo, 11, 5-15.

Barfield, L. H., 1975, Vasi campaniformi della Valpadana: attribuzioni cronologiche e culturali. Atti Simp. Intern. sull' antica eta del Bronzo in Europa, Verona-Lazise, 1972.

Barfield, L. H., 1976a, The cultural affinities of Bell Beakers in Italy and Sicily. Glockenbecher Symposion, Oberried 1974.

Barfield, L. H. and B. Bagolini, 1976b, The excavations on the Rocca di Rivoli, Verona 1963-1968 (Verona).

Barfield, L. H., M. Cremaschi and L. Castelletti, 1975, Stanziamenti del vaso campaniforme a Sant' Ilario d' Enza (Reggio Emilia). Preistoria Alpina 11.

Barfield, L. H., and L. Fasani, 1972, Bemerkungen zum späten Neolithikum und zum Beginn der Bronzezeit in Norditalien. Musaica (Bratislava) XXIII, 45-63.

Barker, G., 1975, The fauna from Monte Covolo. Annali del Museo di Gavardo 11.

Biagi, P., and G. Marchello, 1970, Scavi nella cavernetta Ca' dei Grii (Virle-Brescia). Riv. Sc. Preist. XXV, 253-299.

Clarke, D. L., 1970, The beaker pottery of Great Britain and Ireland (Cambridge).

Colini, G. A., 1898-1902, Il sepolcreto di Remedello sotto nel Bresciano ed il periodo eneolitico in Italia. Bull. Paletn. Ital. XXIV-XXVIII, (serialised article).

Colini, G. A., 1899, Sepolcri eneolitici del Bresciano e del Cremonese. Bull. Paletn. Ital. XXV, 28-32.

Colonna, G., 1970, Fosso Conicchio (Viterbo). Nuovi tesori dell' antica Tuscia: Catalogo della mostra, Viterbo.

Laviosa Zambotti, P., 1939-40. La ceramica della Lagozza e la civiltà palafitticola italiana vista nei suoi rapporti con le civiltà mediterranee ed Europee. Bull. Paletn. Ital. NS III, 61-112, NS IV, 83-164.

Marconi-Bovio, I., 1963, Sulla diffusione dei bicceri campaniformi in Sicilia. Kokalos IX, 106.

Perini, R., 1972, Il deposito secondario n. 3 dei Montesei di Serso. Preistoria Alpina 8, 7-30.

Peroni, R., 1962-63, La Romita di Asciano (Pisa). Bull. Paletn. Ital. 71-72, 251-442.

Peroni, R., 1971, L'età del bronzo nella peninsola italiana, I: L'antica età del bronzo (Firenze).

Ridgway, D., 1972, Beakers in Central Italy. Antiquity XLVI, 52.

Scarani, R., 1962, Gli scavi nella Tanaccia di Brisighella. Preistoria dell' Emilia e Romagna, vol. I, 253-285.

Van der Waals, D. and Glasbergen, W., 1955, Beaker Types and their distribution in the Netherlands. Palaeohistoria iv, 5-46.

Zorzi, F., 1953, Resti di un abitato capannicolo eneolitico alle Colombare di Negrar. Actes du IV Congres Internationale du Quaternaire.

Fig. 2:1   Distribution of Beaker sites in Italy and Sicily

1.	Montesei	28.	Grotta Pollera
2.	La Sassina	29.	Arma delle Anime
3.	Fanè	30.	Sant'Ilario
4.	Le Colombare	31.	Rubiera
5.	Nasa	32.	Bismantova
6.	Praelle di Novaglie	33.	Pescale
6.	Monte Madarosa	34.	Borgo Panigale
8.	Rocca di Rivoli	35.	La Romita di Asciano
9.	Rocci di Garda	36.	Tanaccia di Brisighella
10.	Rocca di Manerba	37.	Grotta del Fontino
11.	Monte Covolo	38.	Fosso Conicchio
12.	Ca' dei Grii	39.	Grotta del Angelo, Olevano
13.	Val Listrea	40.	Grotta Palombara
14.	Sant' Anna, Brescia	41.	Manfria
15.	Buco del Corno	42.	Naro
16.	Trescore Balenare	43.	Serraferlicchio
17.	Isolino	44.	Ribera
18.	Angera	45.	San Bertolo
19.	Monate	46.	Santa Margherita Belice
20.	Legnanello	47.	Manicalunga
21.	Ca' di Marco	48.	Torrebigini
22.	Santa Cristina	49.	Motya
23.	Remedello	50.	Carini
24.	Roccolo Bresciani	51.	Villafrati
25.	Loreto	52.	Grotta Geraci
26.	Grotta del Pertusello	53.	Grotta Puleri
27.	Arma di Nasino		

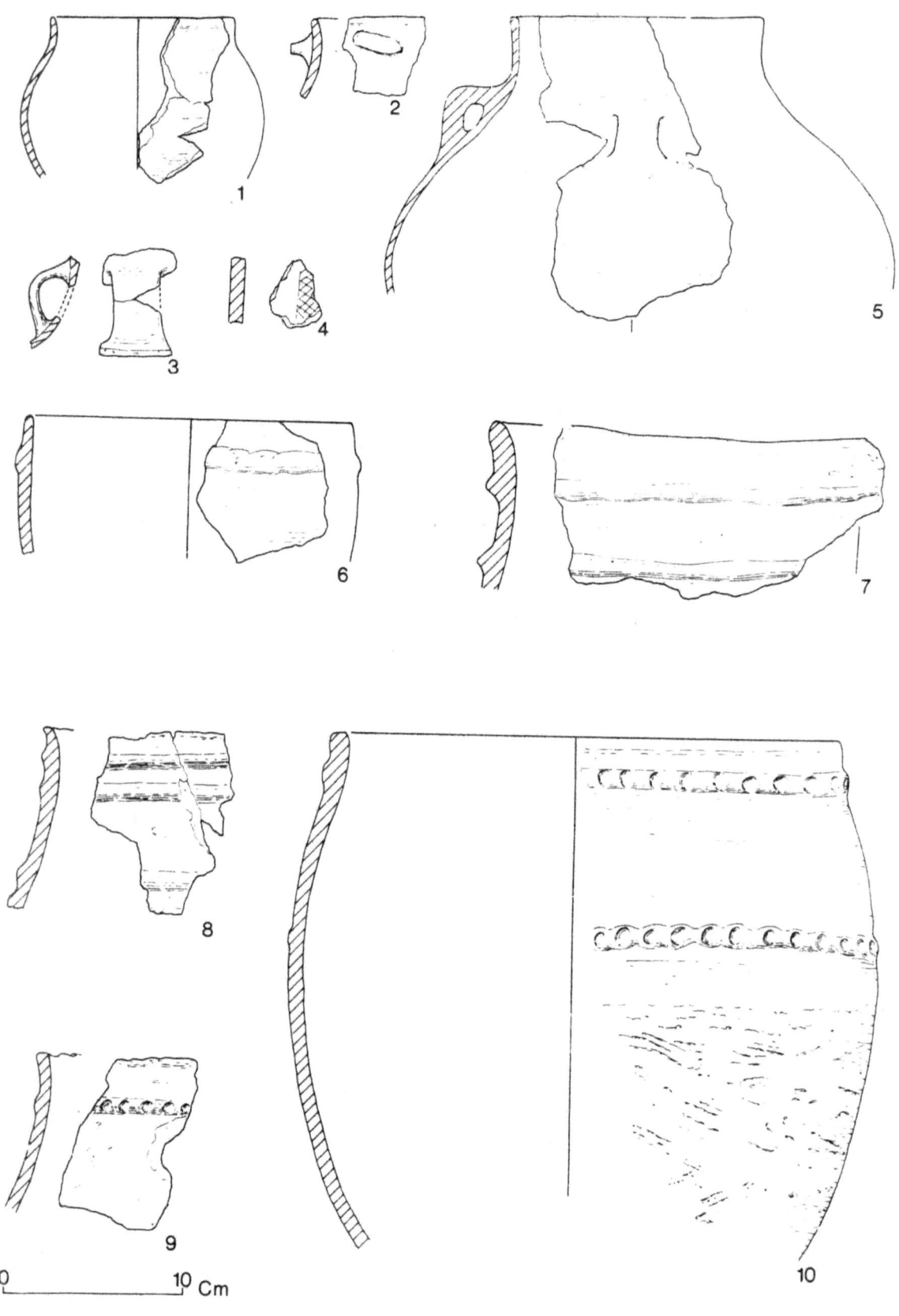

Fig. 2:2 'Begleitkeramik' from Monte Covolo

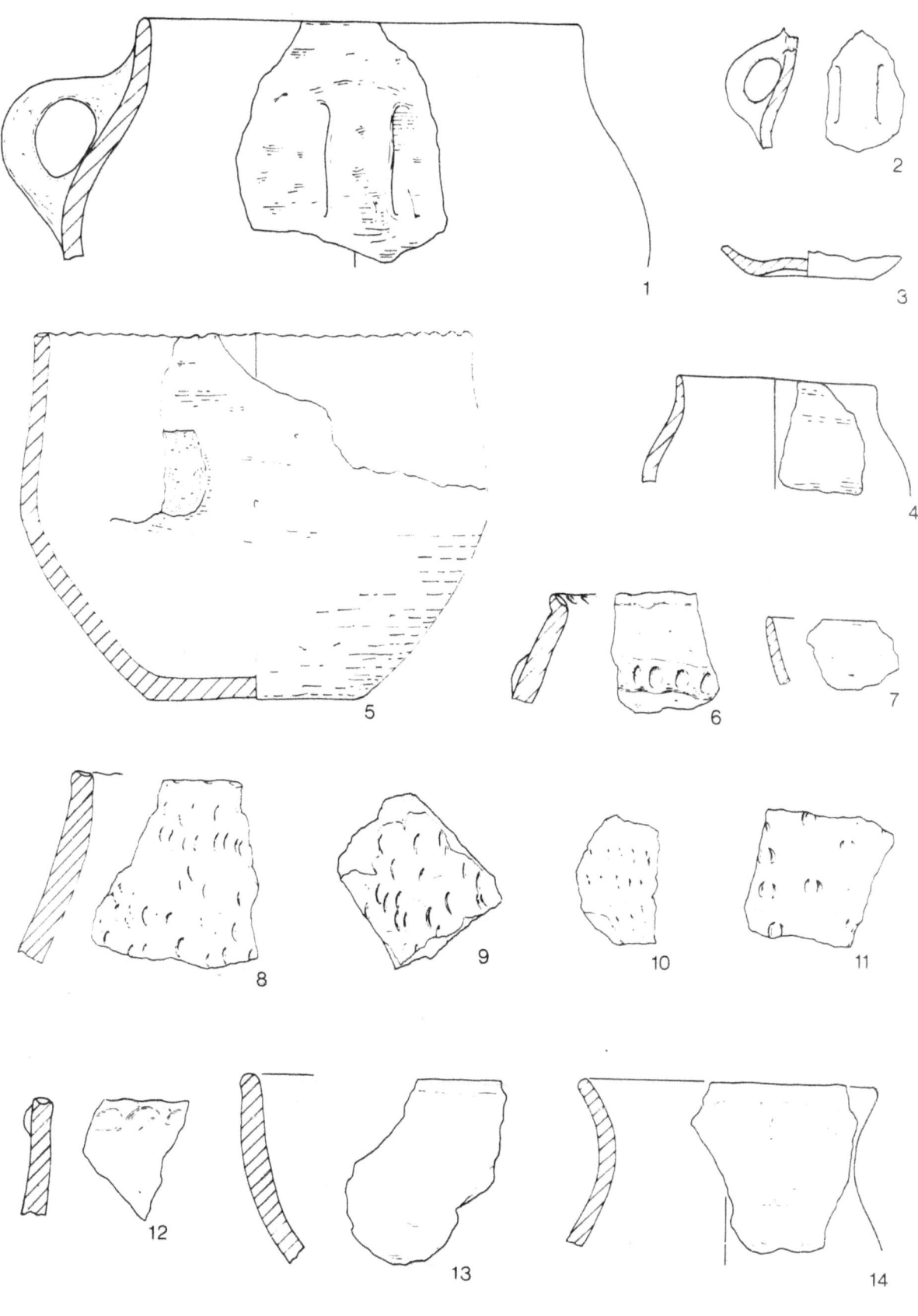

Fig. 2:3   'Begleitkeramik' from S. Ilario

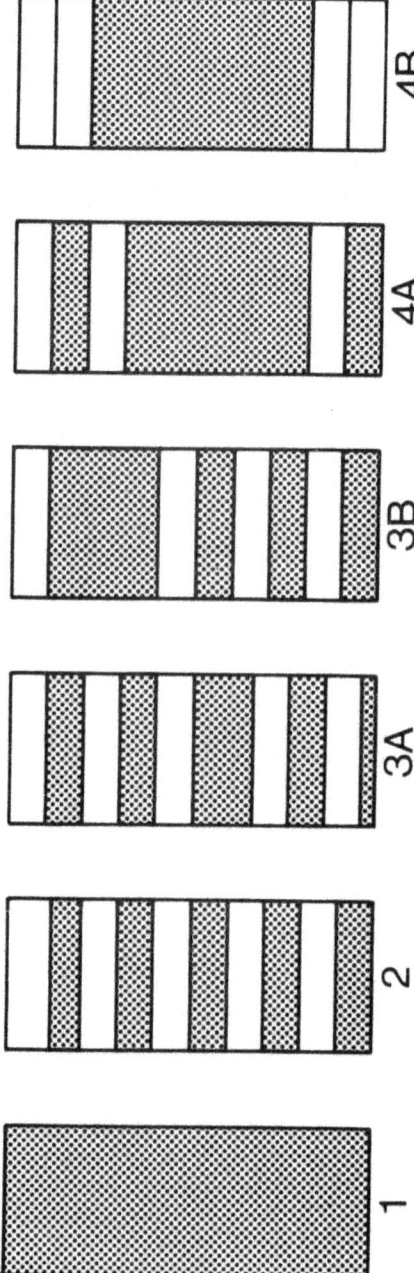

Fig. 2:4 Modes of zone decoration on Italian Beakers

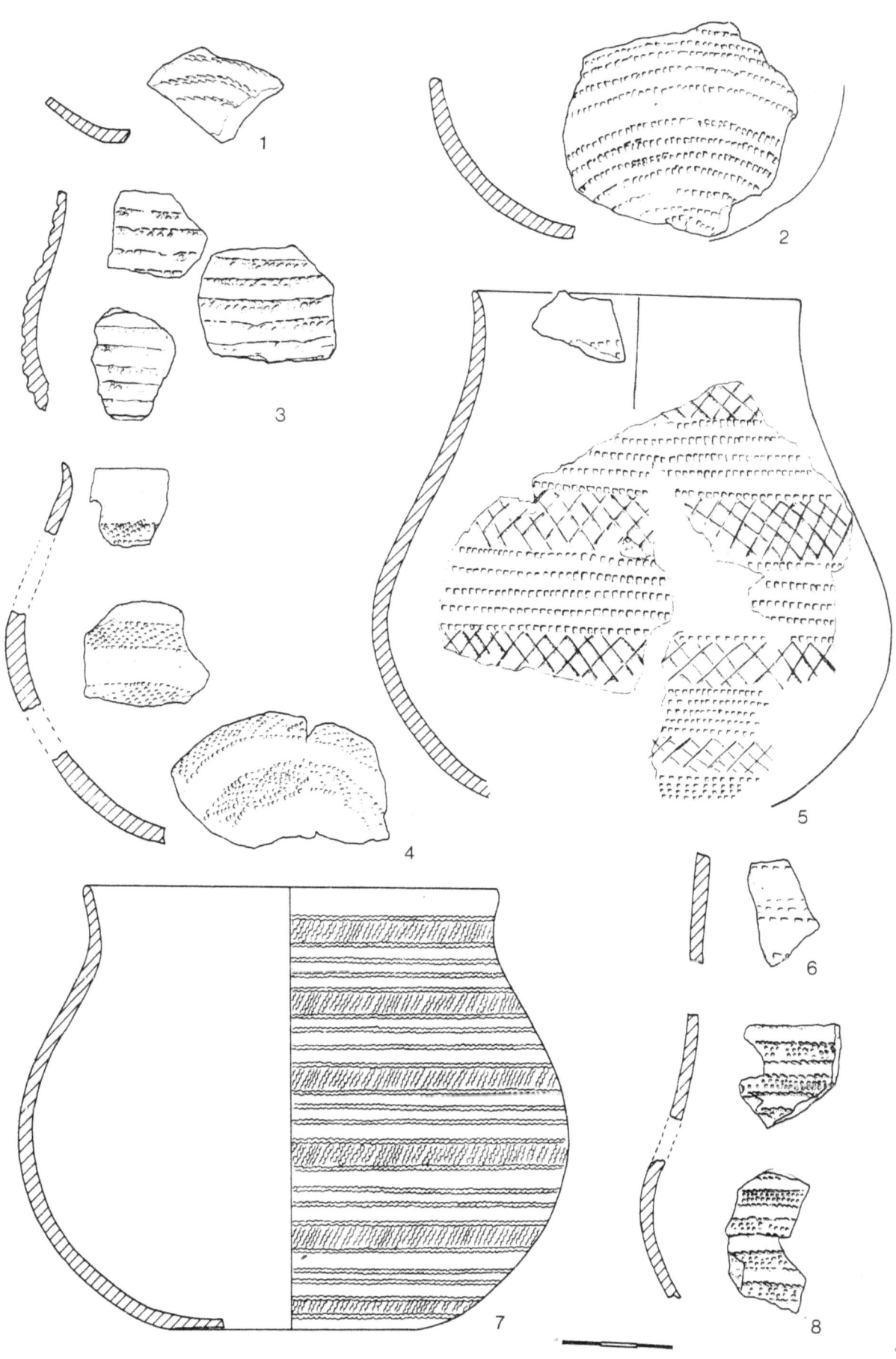

Fig. 2:5 Beakers from Monte Covolo

Fig. 2:6   Beakers from Monte Covolo

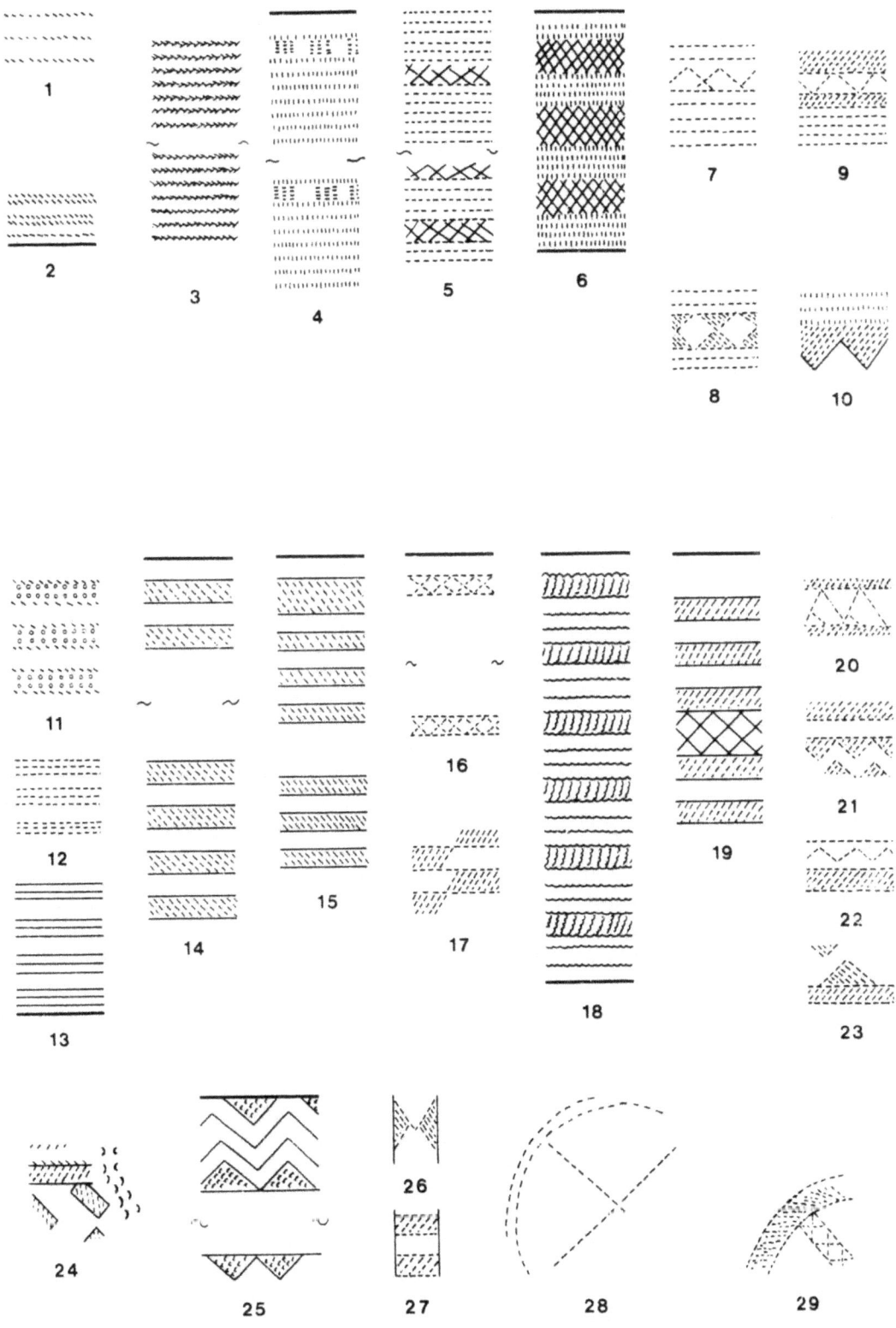

Fig. 2:7   Beaker motifs from Monte Covolo

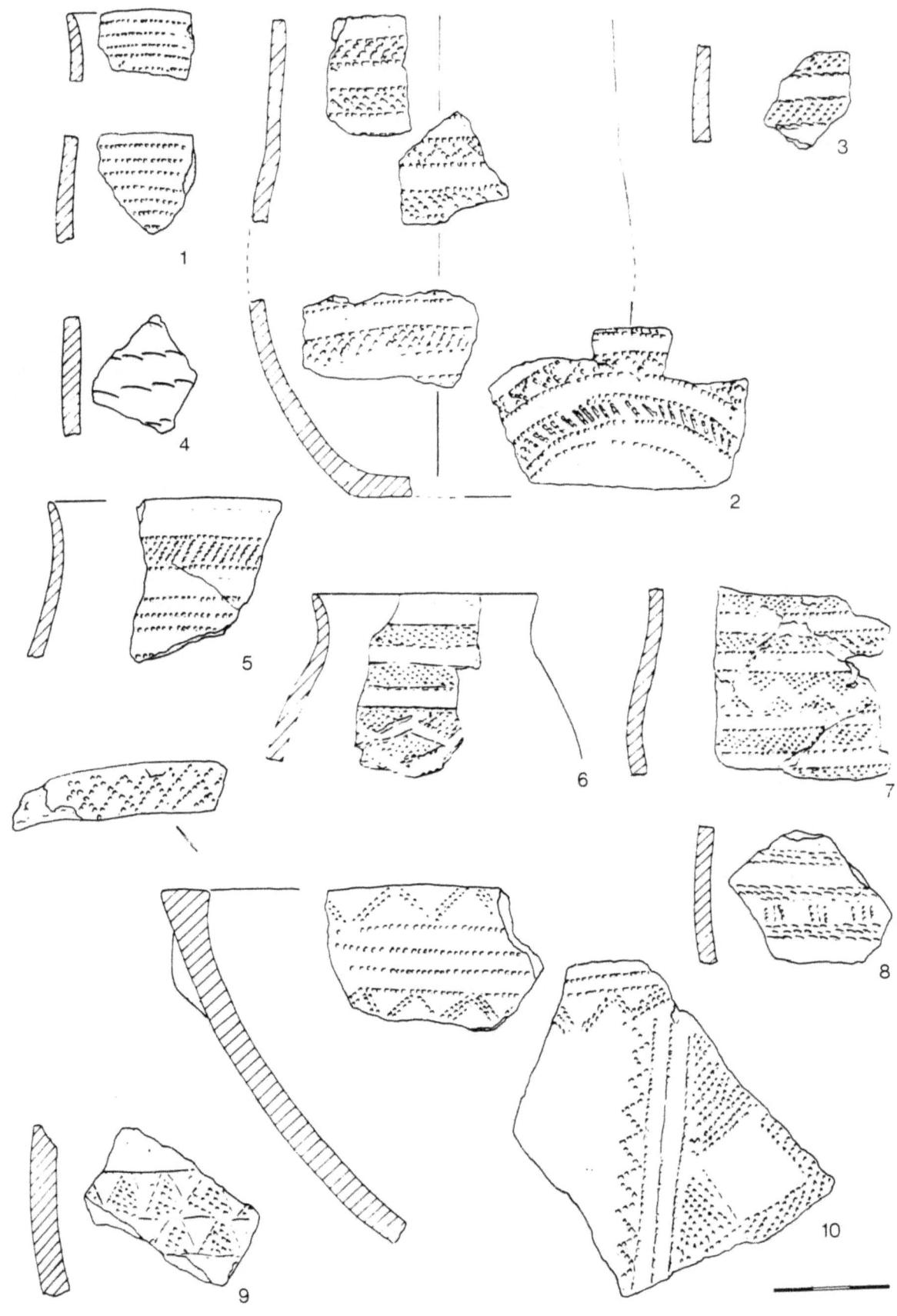

Fig. 2:8   Beakers from Sant' Ilario

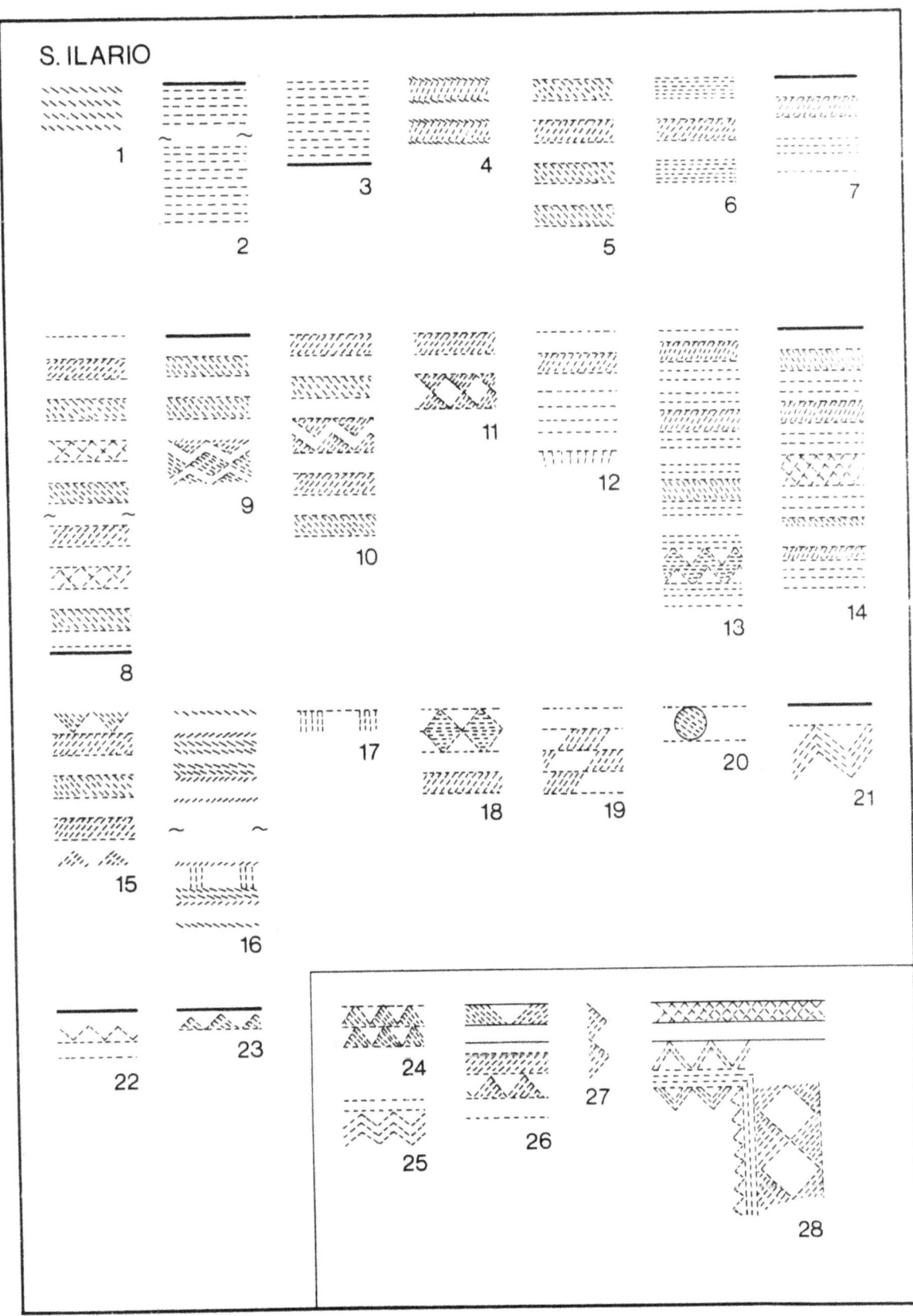

Fig. 2:9 Beaker motifs from Sant' Ilario

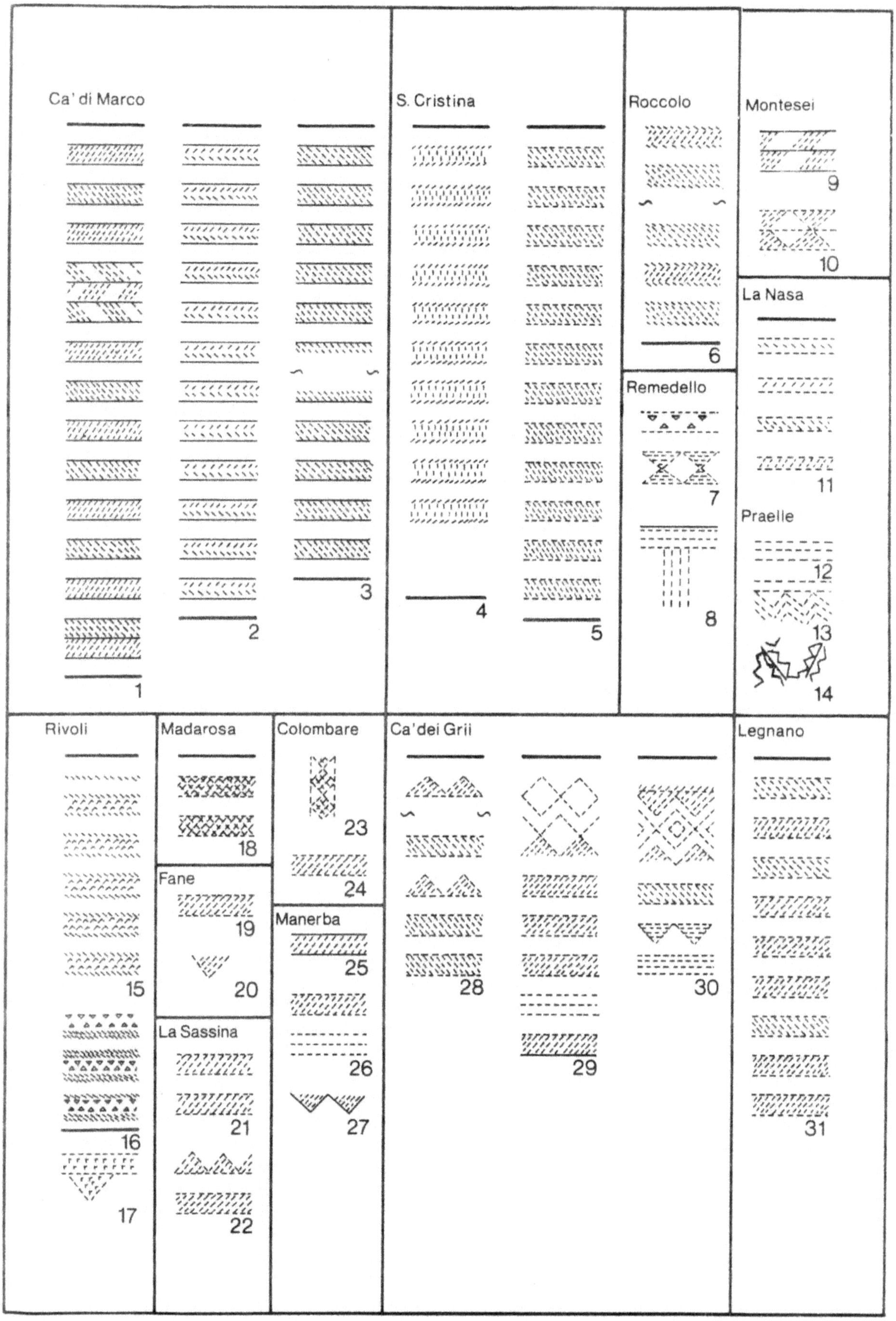

Fig. 2:10 Beaker motifs from the Veneto and Lombardy

46

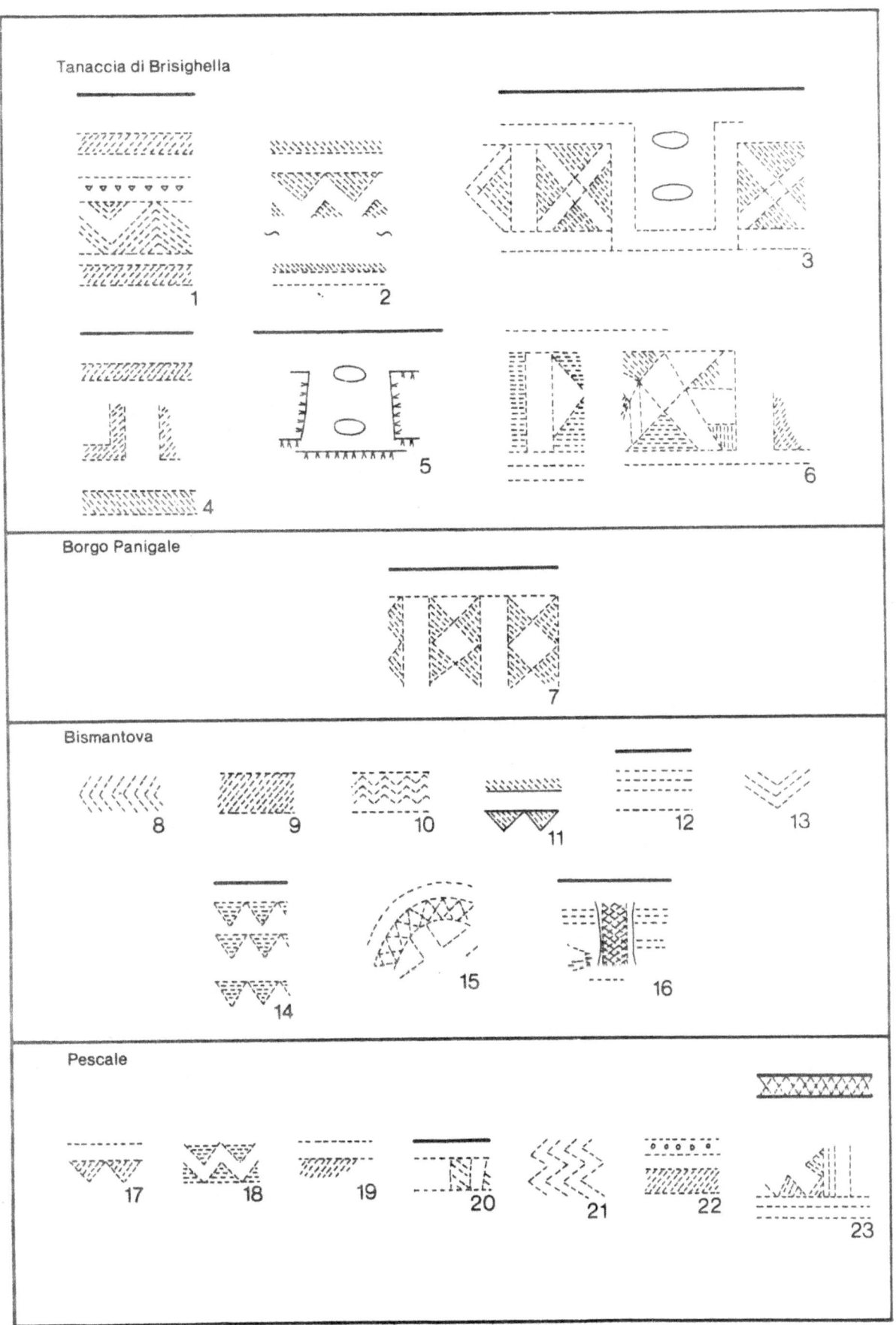

Fig. 2:11 Beaker motifs from Emilia

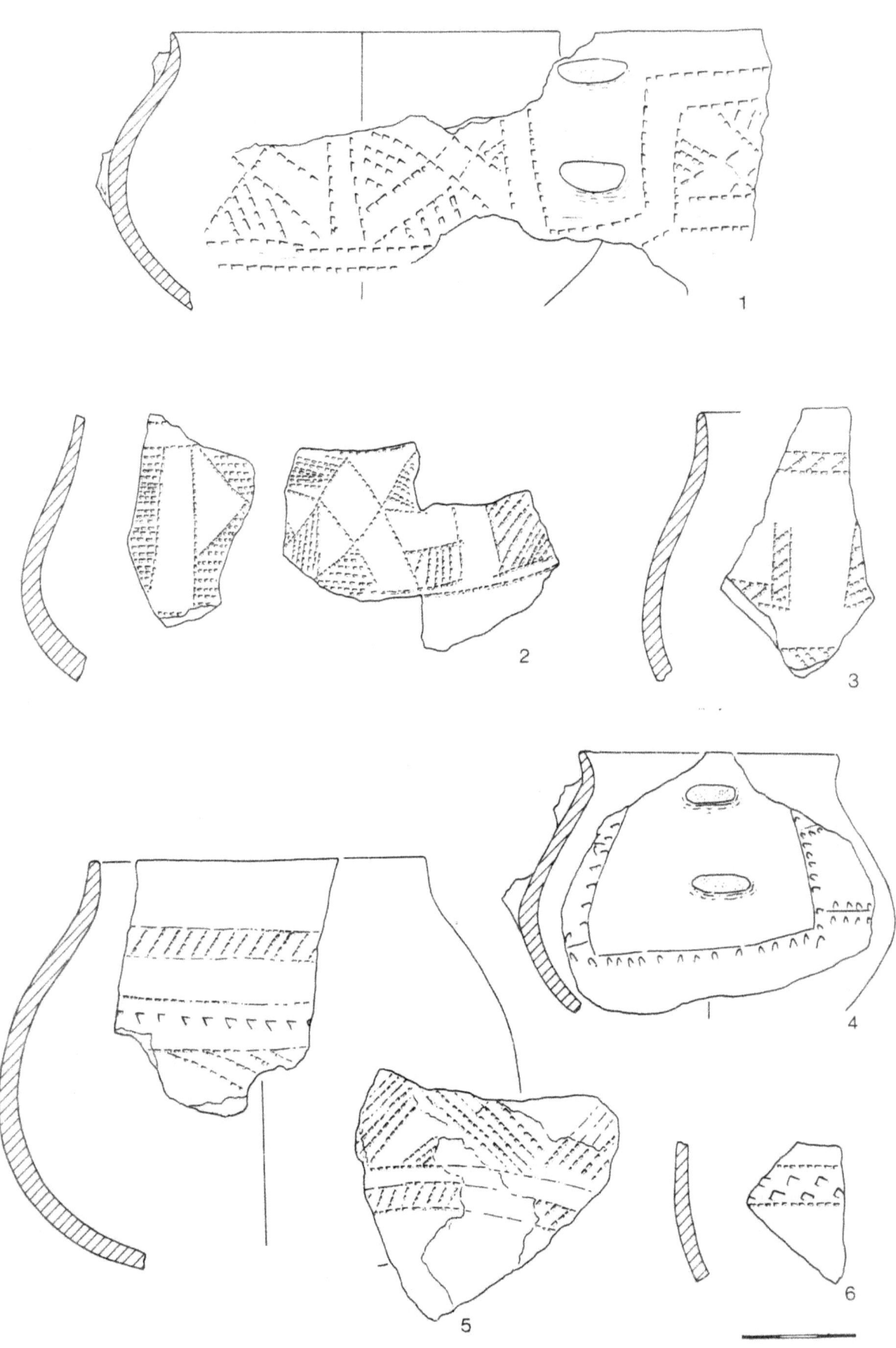

Fig. 2:12 Beakers from Tanaccia di Brisighella

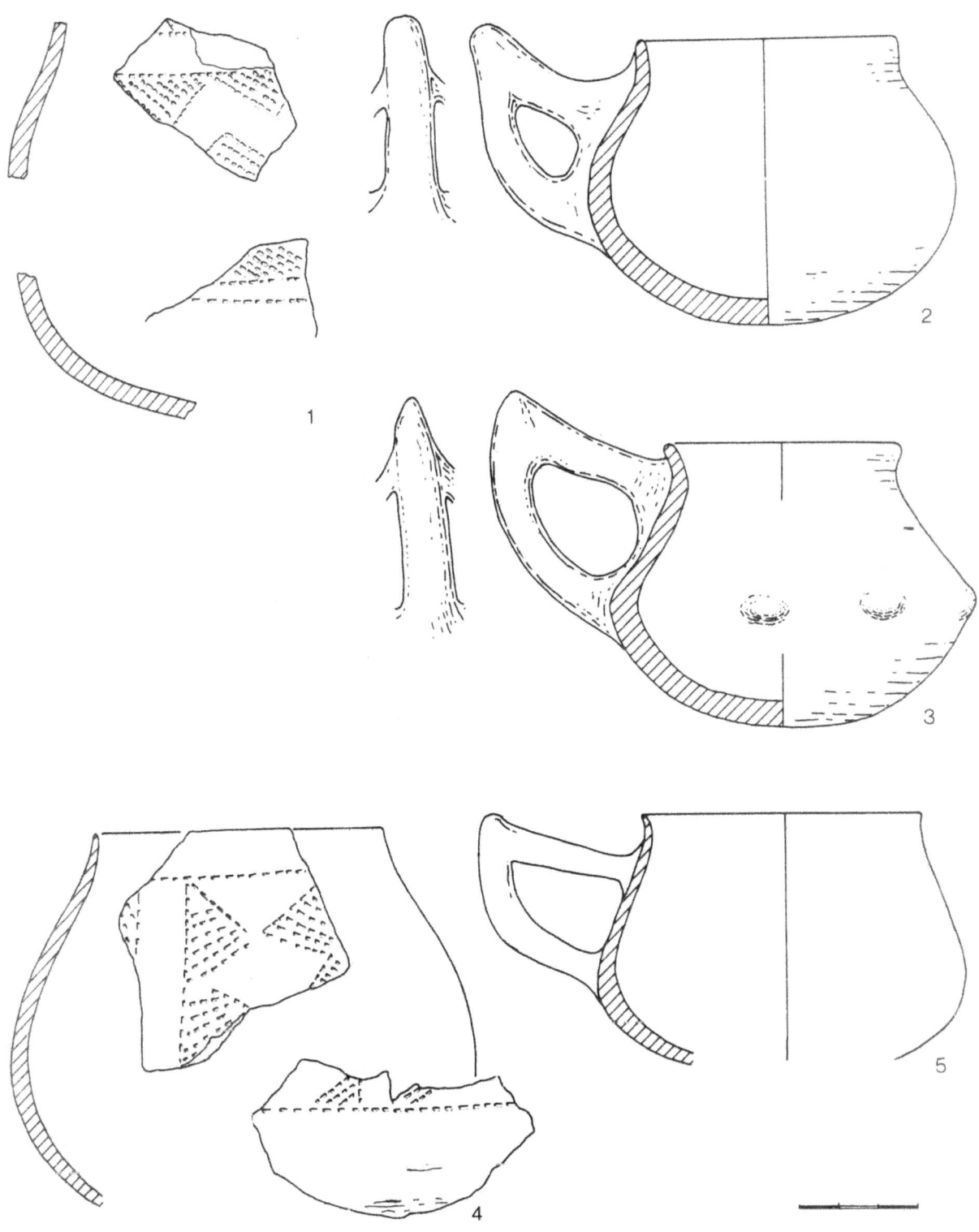

Fig. 2:13 1-3 Beaker and <u>Begleitkeramik</u> from Tanaccia di Brisighella;
4, 5 Beaker and <u>Begleitkeramik</u> from Borgo Panigale

3. THE APPEARANCE OF THE BELL BEAKER ASSEMBLAGE IN CENTRAL EUROPE

S. J. Shennan

The Bell Beaker groups of Central Europe east of the Rhine have remained remarkably little known to western European prehistorians despite a long tradition of research going back to the discovery of Bell Beakers in Moravia, Hungary and elsewhere in the second half of the nineteenth century. Probably the two main reasons for this lack of knowledge are the language difficulties, and the fact that a great deal of the material has still not been satisfactorily published. Since this is the case, a brief characterisation of the assemblage is appropriate.

It is different from that further west in several respects, not least the well-known tendency for Beaker decoration to be heavier than on early beakers further west, and the presence of a range of pottery accompanying the Bell Beakers which includes cups, jugs and conical thickened rim bowls, generally in dark grey burnished fabrics (see Figs. 3:1 and 3:2). In Bohemia the decorated Bell Beakers form 11% of more than 1600 vessels in funerary contexts (which here and throughout Central Europe constitute the main source of finds), while in Moravia the figure is 17% of more than 2100 vessels. Thus only a small proportion of the densely packed dots in the Bohemian and Moravian areas of published Bell Beaker distribution maps actually represent Bell Beakers in the west European sense. With this essential point established, the chronological position of the Bell Beaker assemblage can be described (see Fig. 3:6).

This is best known in the Budapest area of the Carpathian Basin, where the Makó group (related to the Vučedol culture) is succeeded by an assemblage of pottery typologically transitional to that of the classic Early Bronze Age Nagyrév culture, associated with small numbers of decorated Bell Beakers.

Further north-west the position is less clear, but at present the evidence suggests that in Moravia the Bell Beakers follow the Jevišovice B and later Corded Ware groups and are succeeded by the proto-Únětice phase, with a similar sequence in Bohemia: Řivnáč - late Corded Ware - Bell Beakers - proto-Únětice.

In Central Germany (the Saale area) the chronological equivalent of the Řivnáč is the Bernburg culture; this too is succeeded by the Corded Ware, the late phase of which, the Mansfeld phase, may be contemporary with the Bell Beakers, although this is not certain. Again the Bell Beakers are followed by the local Únětice Early Bronze Age.

Within this general chronological framework, it is necessary to consider the question of subdivisions within the Bell Beaker phase in Central

Europe. The marked typological uniformity of the decorated Bell Beakers, and indeed the other vessels as well, suggests that it was short-lived. Although this might merely be interpreted as a reflection of conservatism and/or a lack of stimulus to change, it makes a sharp contrast with the developments seen in both the Netherlands and Britain, which are known to have had a long period in which Bell Beakers were current. The suggestion is confirmed by the available radiocarbon dates. Nevertheless, subdivisions have been proposed, and Hájek's scheme in particular has become widely prevalent (Hájek 1966). According to this there are three phases: in the first, earlier types of decorated Bell Beaker were put in the graves and other varieties of pottery are not found; in the second, later varieties of Bell Beaker were in use, together with other types of accompanying pottery, and finally, the decorated Bell Beakers die out and only the accompanying pottery occurs. Not only is this view based on unacceptable assumptions about the nature of the Bell Beaker assemblage, but the evidence is against it. The single grave stratigraphy known shows the converse of this scheme, with a decorated Bell Beaker later than a jug and other vessels, while further information comes from a consideration of the settlement contexts.

In the Budapest settlements Bell Beakers and proto-Nagyrév pottery are consistently found together; it is only later phases of the Nagyrév culture which are not associated with Bell Beakers. In Moravia decorated Bell Beakers are found together with the various jugs, bowls and jars in 19 pits out of 24 known, representing 20 sites; of the remaining 5 pits, 4 contain very few sherds at all. Moreover, at the sites for which numbers of sherds are given, decorated Bell Beakers are in a minority: there is no suggestion of a 'pure' Bell Beaker culture gradually being 'infiltrated' by local elements, as the traditional view would have it. In Bohemia only 3 of the 14 definite settlement sites recorded do not contain decorated Bell Beaker sherds. Although not conclusive, this evidence certainly does not give much support to the idea of a post-decorated Bell Beaker phase, especially given the relative rarity of Bell Beakers.

Finally, computerised typological studies of the accompanying pottery indicated that no distinctions could be made between those vessels which were found associated with decorated Bell Beakers and those which were not. When this result is taken together with the settlement evidence, it favours the view that those graves which contain decorated Bell Beakers and those which contain only accompanying pottery are not chronologically distinguishable. In fact, it is possible to show that there are other features with which the presence/absence of the Beaker does actually correlate.

As a first step in this procedure, a cluster analysis was carried out on the objects found in the graves, to discover which of these tended to be most frequently associated. A variety of clustering methods was used and all produced essentially similar results, giving one definite cluster consisting of the decorated Bell Beaker, the arrowhead, the stone axe, the flint flake, the copper dagger, the wrist-guard, the earring, the flint scraper, the boar's tusk and the whetstone. The other objects did not form such a definite group.

It was established that spatial factors were not responsible for this grouping and we have already seen that chronology is unlikely to be relevant.

The nature of the objects included in the cluster suggested that it might have prestige significance, and that graves containing them might well be those of individuals of higher rank. Such an interpretation was confirmed by the fact that the mean number of goods in the graves containing these objects was greater than in those without them. Next the relationship between the presence of these goods and the age and sex of the individual buried with them was examined. It appeared that children were less likely than adults to have decorated Bell Beakers or any of the other goods in the cluster; their graves also contained less goods than those of some adults. There are, in fact, no great differences among the children's graves, and it may be suggested that children had a different rank from at least some adults, with few or no ornaments and weapons and few decorated Bell Beakers. Only a minority of adults actually have these goods which are not found with children, a point which may indicate that it was only on arrival at adulthood that individuals had the possibility of changing status and achieving further distinctions. Examination of the association between the Bell Beaker cluster goods and the sex and orientation of the skeleton in the grave showed that within the adults they were largely restricted to males.

A similar investigation was carried out on the Bell Beaker graves of Central Germany. Here too some degree of achieved rank limited to adult males was indicated, although the extent of the differences seemed smaller than in Bohemia and Moravia.

If such objects as the decorated Bell Beaker, copper dagger, wristguard, whetstones etc. were connected with the symbolising of status in these areas, what effect does this have when we turn to the larger scale problems posed by the Bell Beakers and their distribution? It is essentially these artifacts which link the Bell Beaker groups of Central Europe to those of Western Europe, since the domestic assemblages of these areas are basically local, and it is this link which must be the focus of attention if we are trying to explain the unusual features of the Bell Beaker distribution. Here the chronological conclusions presented earlier become important.

Although it had long been recognised that much of the pottery in Central Europe was different from that further west, it was assumed that this was a result of the later differentiation of an originally uniform culture which had been transferred wholesale from one area to another: the preceding analysis suggests this is unlikely. The decorated Bell Beaker may have become differentiated in this way, but the chronological evidence indicates that it appeared in the context of an already existing ceramic assemblage of jugs, cups, bowls etc., and that this assemblage was not a later development.

Given this situation, it seems unnecessary to postulate a population influx into Central Europe, and this view is not contradicted by the physical anthropological evidence (see e.g. Grimm 1969, Bach, Bach and Simon 1972). There is indeed an increasing amount of evidence that the tendency to brachycephaly, which is characteristic of many of the populations found buried with Bell Beakers and their accompanying pottery, may be associated with other traits conferring an adaptive advantage in certain circumstances (see e.g. Olivier and Almeida 1972), resulting in the spread of this feature without any movement of population (see e.g. Coon 1939, p 560.). But if doubt is cast on the association between the spread of Bell Beakers and population movement this only makes it the more important to define precisely those aspects apart from the physical anthropology in which the appearance of Bell Beakers is associated with a change.

This process was begun with an investigation of the similarity in certain features of social organisation between the Corded Ware and Bell Beaker phases in Bohemia. The Corded Ware graves show a pattern in which there are only small differences in the quantities of goods in children's graves and certain types, particularly ornaments and weapons, are restricted to adults. The Bell Beaker graves of the area show a similar situation in these respects but not in certain others. While females as well as males are found at the top end of the 'wealth' scale in the Corded Ware graves this does not seem to be the case with the Bell Beakers, where the indications are that most of the richer graves are male. Secondly, the shape of the frequency distribution of graves in terms of their numbers of goods is markedly different, (see Fig. 3:3). In the Corded Ware case there is a rectangular block with equal numbers of graves having different amounts of goods, and just a few outliers which do not fit into this pattern, whereas the Bell Beaker graves show a gradual decrease in the number of graves with increasing amounts of goods - more the sort of pyramidal distribution to be expected in a ranked organisation, where it is unusual for the same number to be in a lower as in a higher category. While considering the graves, another feature worth mentioning is the change in the prevailing grave orientation from East-West to North-South, which as Fischer (1975) has said, is so marked as to suggest an intentional opposition; similar changes occur in Corded Ware groups elsewhere (Häusler 1969).

The next aspect to be considered is change in the material assemblage itself. In the past there has been a tendency to dismiss this and say simply that the 'Corded Ware culture' was replaced by the 'Bell Beaker culture'. This may be broadly true, but it is insufficient when we are looking at the process of change from one to the other: for this it is necessary to focus on individual trajectories of change. In particular it is possible to look at changes in vessel morphology. If the bulk of the pottery changes radically, there are different inferences to be drawn than if only a small proportion of fine pottery changes. Especial interest centres on the origin of the Bell Beaker, which several authors have suggested should be sought in Central Europe. Similarities between decorated Bell Beakers and pottery of the Vučedol culture have been very much overemphasised: only the Corded Ware assemblage provides an antecedent vessel which is functionally a beaker, and these are characterised by a horizontally arranged scheme of decoration similar to that of the Bell Beakers, thus it is here, if anywhere in our area, that an origin must be sought.

Four functional vessel types, jugs, bowls, jars and beakers, present in both the Corded Ware and the Bell Beaker inventory, were selected, and vessels from the two assemblages were compared by means of a principal components analysis carried out on measurements of the shape alone so that the results for all the types might be comparable. The analysis showed paradoxically that the change from Corded Ware to Bell Beaker was only really indicated in the beakers themselves, and cannot be regarded as a wholesale break in the pottery tradition of the area. One possible inference from this situation is that the decorated Bell Beaker was an introduction from outside to Central Europe; the argument receives support from the work of Lanting and van der Waals (e.g. 1973) and it will be discussed further below. As far as the other pottery is concerned it should be noted that the jugs, cups and bowls which appear in the Corded Ware assemblage are not present in its earlier phases and represent the adoption of functional vessel categories, probably related to eating and drinking styles, which first appeared in the Carpathian Basin.

Discussion of the changes in the assemblage would not be complete without mention of one of the most obvious contrasts between the two sets of grave goods, that in the prestige male equipment between the Corded Ware polished stone battle-axe and the Bell Beaker copper dagger and wrist-guard. This change seems to have been a very general phenomenon over Central Europe at this time. Finds of both tanged daggers and moulds for their manufacture show that they were already in use in the Carpathian Basin in the Baden period and continued through the Vucedol phase. They appear to be present from the beginning of the Bell Beaker phase in Central Europe but not in the North-West, where Grand-Pressigny flint blades occur in the earliest graves and also in late Protruding Foot Beaker contexts.

The changes just described, however, are in the assemblage itself and in the organisation which its grave associations reflect. These are necessarily the immediate focus of our attention but they are only a small part of the system as a whole and it is essential to examine changes in other dimensions some way removed, which may nevertheless be related to those in which we are mainly interested.

One of the most important of these, and one of the most difficult to assess, is population, although one possible indicator of population increase is expansion of the settled area. This did not take place on a large scale until the Middle-Late Bronze Age; there do seem to be signs of smaller scale infilling in certain areas during the late Neolithic but this occurs at an earlier date than the appearance of Bell Beakers. The same may be said of the marked change in settlement pattern which occurs at the transition from Middle to Late Neolithic in Central Europe. Settlements of the earlier period are comparatively large and densely populated; there is some indication of a settlement hierarchy, with specialised production, and concentration of traded objects in settlements with sometimes quite developed fortifications. On the appearance of the Corded Ware locations change, settlements seem to be smaller and more dispersed, and there is no sign of defences, or of a hierarchy. When the Bell Beaker phase began this dispersed settlement pattern was already established and all the evidence available suggests that the Beaker pattern was exactly the same. The settlement pattern is, of course, one of the reasons why the makers and users of Corded Ware and Bell Beaker pottery have in the past been regarded as nomadic pastoralists. Neustupný (1969), however, has presented cogent arguments for not seeing the Corded Ware in this light and there is no reason why these should not apply to the Bell Beakers as well. Furthermore, the distribution of Bell Beaker sites in relation to the soils shows the basic restriction to the more fertile areas which is apparent throughout the Neolithic (see figs. 3:4 and 3:5).

In the light of these results it is necessary to offer a model for the appearance of Bell Beakers in Central Europe which does not involve change in these dimensions but does explain the similarities between Central and Western Europe which are characteristic of the Bell Beaker period. Some of the widespread objects, such as the tanged copper dagger, are most probably prestige goods wherever they occur, but the same cannot be said for the decorated Bell Beaker, which in some parts of Western Europe is found with virtually everybody who had any goods at all. In these same areas beakers of poorer quality play an important part in the domestic assemblages. This seems to indicate a core area of the type suggested by Clarke (1976), but referring only to the decorated Bell Beaker itself and to nothing else. Such a core area would be an obvious place for the origin of the vessel, as Lanting and van der Waals have suggested (1973). On this view the core region is not in any way remarkable - the interest lies in the fact that a particular element in the assemblage of beaker-type pottery, the fine decorated Bell Beaker, expanded far beyond its original bounds, not least into Central Europe. Other widespread types, like the tanged copper dagger and the wrist-guard, do not originate in the West: they are not present there in the earliest phase as they are in Central Europe, where, as we have seen, their origin is most probably to be found.

It is important to realise that we are not simply dealing with the movement of objects - many were manufactured locally, including decorated Bell Beakers. It is likely, however, that this was a result of the importation into Central Europe of decorated Beakers which were then imitated. If this introduction took place by means of down-the-line reciprocal exchange no single vessel need have moved a very long distance. At least semi-specialist potters are likely to have been involved in the process, manufacturing particularly high quality vessels which attained a relatively widespread distribution and were then copied with inferior techniques and materials.

Why was the pattern of contact associated with the Bell Beakers different from that which preceded it? It seems possible that the diffusion of three important innovations was involved, the spread to the West of the use of the domestic horse and of the technology to exploit more complex copper ores, together with the adoption of the dagger as the prestige weapon. These are all innovations at this time in north-west Europe and their origin lies in the Carpathian Basin and Central Europe generally.

As far as the horse is concerned, the evidence for Western Europe has been presented by van Wijngaarden-Bakker (1974), while Central Europe is dealt with by Bökönyi (e.g. 1974). Of particular interest are the uniquely high proportions of horses at the sites on the Csepel Island near Budapest, where numbers of Bell Beaker sherds are associated with proto-Nagyrév pottery. The other two aspects require little comment: the tanged copper dagger has already been discussed, and the appearance of copper metallurgy in north-west Europe has been thoroughly covered by Case (1969) and Butler and van der Waals (1969).

It is possible that interest in acquiring these innovations led to the establishment of relations oriented in the direction from which they came. These moved westwards while examples of the fine component of a basically Beaker local assemblage were abstracted from their context and moved east. Whether this was because of their intrinsic attractiveness, their contents, or their association with some fashionable drinking custom is unknown; certainly an interest in fine pottery for its own sake should not be considered improbable. The fact that developments in pottery decoration which had occurred in Central Europe began to be taken up later in the West only demonstrates the continuing ceramic contact.

We do not know why the system appeared when it did, or why it should have arisen at all, but one factor which should be borne in mind is the date at which these innovations appeared in the first place. It was only quite late in the Central European Copper Age that the technology for exploiting complex ores such as those found in Western Europe was developed, and extensive use of the domestic horse too seems to have begun in the late Tripolje culture, not so long before the Bell Beakers. The innovations may have actually been taken up because of a trend towards increased ranking: possible evidence might be the appearance of increasingly large henge monuments in Britain at this time, or such rich Bell Beaker graves as Exloo in the Netherlands, while attention has already been drawn to the differing distribution of grave goods in Corded Ware and Bell Beaker graves in Bohemia. Increased ranking may well have led to the creation of a demand for symbolic differentiation which these innovations satisfied - the horse too probably played a social rather than an economic role.

Once the innovations had been widely diffused the need for such contacts would disappear and there would no longer by any compulsion to keep up the network. With the Early Bronze Age the contacts are not lost but clearly grew more sporadic as the local regions became more independent.

BIBLIOGRAPHY

1) General

Butler, J. J. and J. D. van der Waals, 1966, 'Bell Beakers and Early Metal-working in the Netherlands', Palaeohistoria 12: 41-139.

Case, H. J., 1966, 'Were Beaker-people the First Metallurgists in Ireland?', Palaeohistoria 12: 141-177.

Coon, C. S., 1939, The Races of Europe. New York.

Fischer, U., 1975, 'Zur Deutung der Glockenbecherkultur', Nassauische Annalen 86: 1-13.

Hájek, L., 1957, 'Knoflíky středoevropské skupiny zvoncovitých pohárů' (Buttons of the Central European Bell Beaker group), Památky archeologické 48: 389-424.

Hájek, L., 1966, 'Die älteste Phase der Glockenbecherkultur in Böhmen und Mähren', Památky archeologické 57: 210-241.

Häusler, A., 1969, 'Die östlichen Beziehungen der schnurkeramischen Becherkulturen', in Behrens, H. and F. Schlette (eds.) Die neolithischen Becherkulturen im Gebiet der DDR und ihre europäischen Beziehungen: 255-274. Berlin.

Lanting, J. N., W. G. Mook and J. D. van der Waals, 1973, 'C14 Chronology and the Beaker Problem', Helinium 13: 38-58.

Lanting, J. N., and J. D. van der Waals (eds.) 1976, Glockenbecher Symposion Oberried 1974. Bussum/Haarlem.
This volume is the single most important reference to recent work on Bell Beakers throughout Europe. The articles it contains are not listed separately in this bibliography.

Müller-Karpe, H., 1974, Handuch der Vorgeschichte Bd. III: Kupferzeit. Munich.

Neustupný, E., 1969, 'Economy of the Corded Ware Cultures', Archeologické rozhledy 21: 43-68.

Neustupný, E., 1971, 'Factors determining the variability of the Corded Ware Culture', in Renfrew C. (ed.) The Explanation of Culture Change: 725-730. London.

Neustupný, E., 1972, 'Das jungere Äneolithikum im Mitteleuropa', Musaica 12: 91-120.

Olivier, G., and M. E. de Castro Almeida, 1972, 'Forme du Crane et Mortalité differentielle par Tuberculose', L'Anthropologie 76: 471-499.

Pleslová-Štiková, E., 1972, 'Zur Frage der Entstehung und Bedeutung der jungäneolithischen Befestigungen in Mitteleuropa, Musaica 12: 23-43.

Sangmeister, E., 1964, 'Die Glockenbecher im Oberrheintal', Jahrbuch des römisch-germanischen Zentralmuseums Mainz 11: 81-114.

Sangmeister, E., 1972, 'Sozial-ökonomische Aspekte der Glockenbecherkultur', Homo 23: 188-202.

ii) Carpathian Basin

Bóna, I., 1963, 'The Cemeteries of the Nagyrév Culture', Alba Regia 2-3: 11-23.

Kalicz, N., 1968, Die Frühbronzezeit in Nordostungarn. Budapest.

Schreiber, R., 1967, 'Neuere Forschungsergebnisse über die frühe Bronzezeit in der Umgebung von Budapest', A Morá Ferenc Muzeum Evkönyve 1966-7: 63-70.

Schreiber, R., 1972, 'A korabronzkor problémái Budapesten' (Problems of the Early Bronze Age in Budapest), Archaeologiai Értesítő 99: 151-166.

Schreiber, R., 1973, Die Glockenbecherkultur in Budapest, Budapest.

Schreiber, R., 1975, 'Die Bedeutung von Budapest in der Chronologie der mitteleuropäischen Fruhbronzezeit', Acta Archaeologica Carpathica 15: 163-172.

Točík, A., 1961, 'Stratigraphie auf der befestigten Ansiedlung in Malé Kosihy, Bez. Štúrovo, in Točík, A. (ed) Kommission für das Äneolithikum und die ältere Bronzezeit: 17-38. Bratislava.

iii) Moravia

Medunová-Benesová, A., 1972, Jevišovice-Starý Zámek, Schicht B - Katalog der Funde. Brno.

Ondráček, J., 1967, 'Moravská protoúnetická kultura' (The Moravian Proto-Únetice Culture), Slovenska Archaeologia 15: 389-446.

Pavelčík, J., 1973, 'Befestigte Industriezentren der Träger der Badener Kultur und ihr Platz in der gesellschaftlich-ökonomischen Entwicklung des ostlichen Teiles Mitteleuropas', Musaica 13: 41-62.

iv) Bohemia

Buchvaldek, M., 1967, Die Schnurkeramik in Böhmen. Prague.

Buchvaldek, M., and D. Koutecký 1970, Vikletice, Ein schnurkeramisches Gräberfeld, Prague.

Buchvaldek, M., and D. Koutecký, 1972, 'Die Interpretation des schnurkeramischen Gräberfeldes von Vikletice', Památky archeologické 63: 142-179.

Ehrich, R. W., and Pleslová-Štiková E., 1968, Homolka, an Eneolithic site in Bohemia, Prague and Cambridge, Mass.

Hájek, L., 1966, 'La civilisation des vases companiformes', in Filip, J., (ed.) Investigations archeologiques en Tchecoslovaquie: 101-106. Prague.

Hájek, L., 1968, Die Glockenbecherkultur in Böhmen, Prague.

Kytlicová, O., 1960, 'Eneolitické pohřebiště v Brandýsku' (An Eneolithic Cemetery at Brandysek), Památky archeologické 51: 442-474.

Moucha, V., 1963, 'Die Periodisierung der Úneticer Kultur in Böhmen', Sborník Československé společnosti archeologické 3: 9-60.

Neustupný, E., 1965, 'Hrob z Tušimic a některé problémy kultur se šňůrovou keramikou' (The grave at Tušimice and some problems of the Corded Ware Culture), Památky archeologické 56: 392-452.

Pleslová-Štiková, E., 1972, 'Eneolitické Osídlení v Lysolajích u Prahy' (An Eneolithic Settlement at Lysolaje near Prague), Památky archeologické 63: 3-141.

Stocký, A., 1929, La Bohême prehistorique I, L'Age de pierre.

Zápotocký, M., 1960, 'Sídliště kultury zvoncovitých pohárů u Kozel na Neratovicku' (A Bell Beaker settlement at Kozly), Památky archeologické 51: 5-26.

v) Central Germany

Bach, A., H. Bach and K. Simon, 1972, 'Anthropologische Aspekte der Bevölkerungsentwicklung im westlichen Mitteldeutschland', Jahresschrift für mitteldeutsche Vorgeschichte 56: 7-38.

Behrens, H., 1973 Die Jungsteinzeit im Mittelelbe-Saale-Gebiet, Berlin

Fischer, C., 1959, 'Die Keramik der Mansfelder Gruppe', Jahresschrift für mitteldeutsche Vorgeschichte 43: 136-187.

Fischer, U., 1956, Die Gräber der Steinzeit im Saalegebiet, Berlin

Gerhardt, K., 1953, Die Glockenbecherleute in Mittel-und Westdeutschland. Stuttgart.

Grimm, H., 1969, 'Kenntnisse und Forschungslücken in der Anthropologie der Becherkulturen auf dem Gebiet der DDR', in Behrens, H. and F. Schlette (eds.) Die Neolithischen Becherkulturen im Gebiet der DDR und ihre europaischen Beziehungen: 197-208, Berlin.

Kaufmann, D., 1967, 'Die jungsteinzeitlichen Besiedlung am unteren Bodelauf unter Berücksichtigung siedlungskundlicher Probleme', Jahresschrift für mitteldeutsche Vorgeschichte 51: 89-110.

Mania, D., 1972, 'Zur spät- und nacheiszeitlichen Landschaftsgeschichte des mittleren Elb-Saalegebietes', Halle Jahrbuch für Mitteldeutsche Erdgeschichte 11: 7-36.

Matthias, W., 1969, 'Die Schnurkeramik in westlichen Mitteldeutschland', in Behrens, H., and F. Schlette (eds.) Die neolithischen Becherkulturen im Gebiet der DDR und ihre europäischen Beziehungen: 9-28. Berlin.

Neumann, G., 1929, 'Die Gliederung der Glockenbecherkultur im mitteldeutschland', Prähistorische Zeitschrift 20: 3-69.

Neumann, G., 1969, 'Die Glockenbecherkultur im Spiegel einiger thüringischer Siedlungsplätze', in Behrens, H. and F. Schlette (eds.) Die neolithische Becherkulturen im Gebiet der DDR und ihre europäischen Beziehungen: 131-142. Berlin.

Schlabow, K., 1959, 'Beiträge zur Erforschung der jungsteinzeitlichen und bronzezeitlichen Gewebetechnik Mitteldeutschlands', Jahresschrift für mitteldeutsche Vorgeschichte 43: 101-120.

Schlette, F., 1948, 'Die neuen Funde der Glockenbecherkultur im Lande Sachsen-Anhalt', Strena Praehistorica: 29-77.

Scultze-Motel, J., 1969, 'Kulturpflanzenfunde der Becherkulturen', in Behrens, H., and F. Schlette (eds.) Die neolithischen Becherkulturen im Gebiet der DDR und ihre europäischen Beziehungen: 169-172. Berlin.

Shennan, S. J., and J. D. Wilcock, 1975 'Shape and style variation in Central German Bell Beakers: a computer assisted study', Science and Archaeology 15: 17-31.

vi) Poland

Kamieńska, J. and A. Kulczycka-Leciejewiczowa, 1964, 'Quelques remarques sur la civilisation des vases campaniformes en Pologne', Archaeologia Polona 7: 96-113.

Kamieńska, J. and A. Kulczycka-Leciejewiczowa, 1970, 'The Bell Beaker Culture', in Wiślański T. (ed.) The Neolithic in Poland: Wrocław-Warszawa-Kraków.

Kruk, J., 1973, Studia osadnice nad neolitem wyżyn lessowych (Studies of Neolithic settlement on the loess uplands). Wrocław-Warszawa-Kraków.

Krzak, Z., 1976, The Złota Culture. Wrocław-Warszawa-Kraków.

Wojciechowski, W., 1972, 'Uwagi o kulturze pucharów dzwonowatych na Dolnym Śląsku' (Remarks on the Bell Beaker culture in Lower Silesia), Silesia Antiqua 14: 33-65.

vii) The Horse

Bökönyi, S., 1968, 'Die Wirbeltierfauna der Siedlung von Salgótarján-Pécskö', Acta Archaeologica Hungarica 20:59-100.

Bökönyi, S., 1971, 'The development and history of domestic animals in Hungary: the Neolithic through the Middle Ages', American Anthropologist 73: 640-674.

Bökönyi, S., 1974, The History of Domestic Mammals in Central and Eastern Europe. Budapest.

Clason, A., 1969, 'Einige Bemerkungen uber Viehzucht, Jagd und Knochenbearbeitung bei der mitteldeutschen Schnurkeramik', in Behrens, H. and F. Schlette (Eds.) Die neolithischen Becherkulturen im Gebiet der DDR und ihre europäischen Beziehungen 173-195. Berlin.

Schüle, W., 1969, 'Glockenbecher und Hauspferde', in Boessneck, J. (ed.) Archäologie und Biologie: 88-93. Wiesbaden.

Wijngaarden-Bakker, L. H. van, 1974, 'The animal remains from the Beaker settlement at Newgrange, Co. Meath: First Report', Proceedings of the Royal Irish Academy, 74C: 313-383.

NOTE: Those articles with a Czech or Polish title and an English translation in parentheses have either an English or German summary.

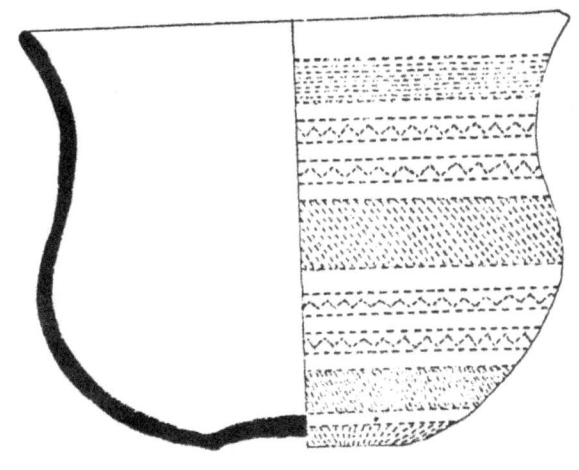
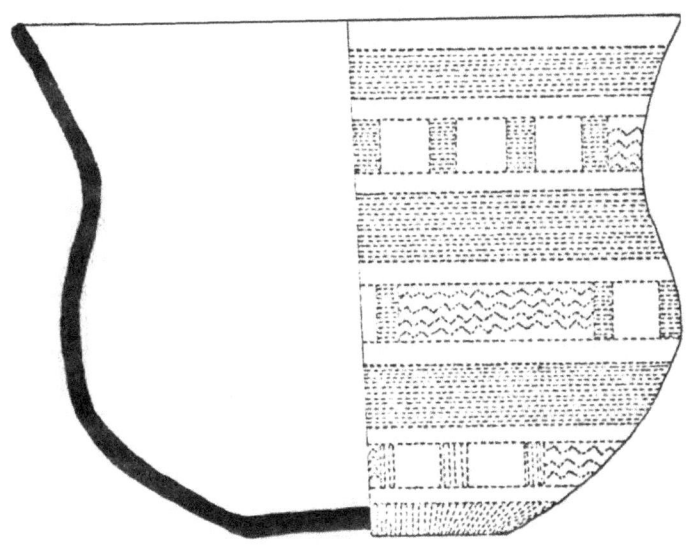
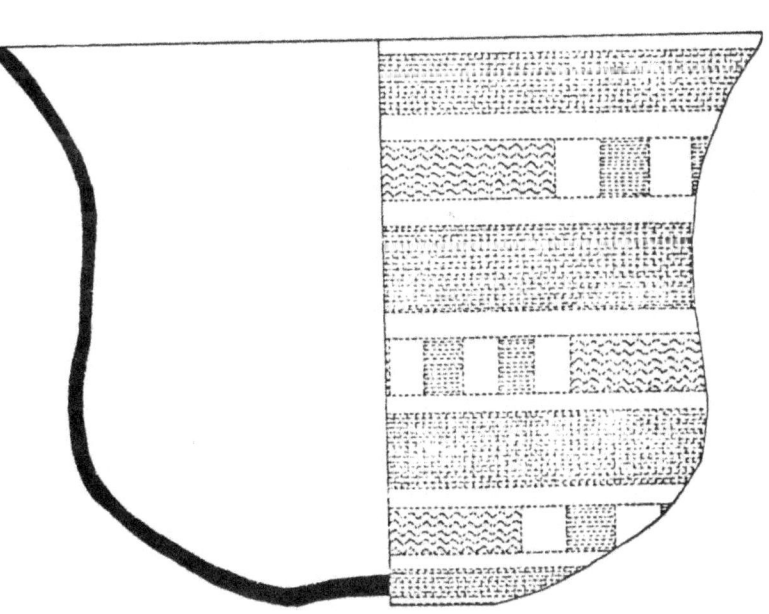

Fig. 3:1 Examples of Bell Beakers from Bohemia.
Scale: top two 3:8; bottom 1:2.

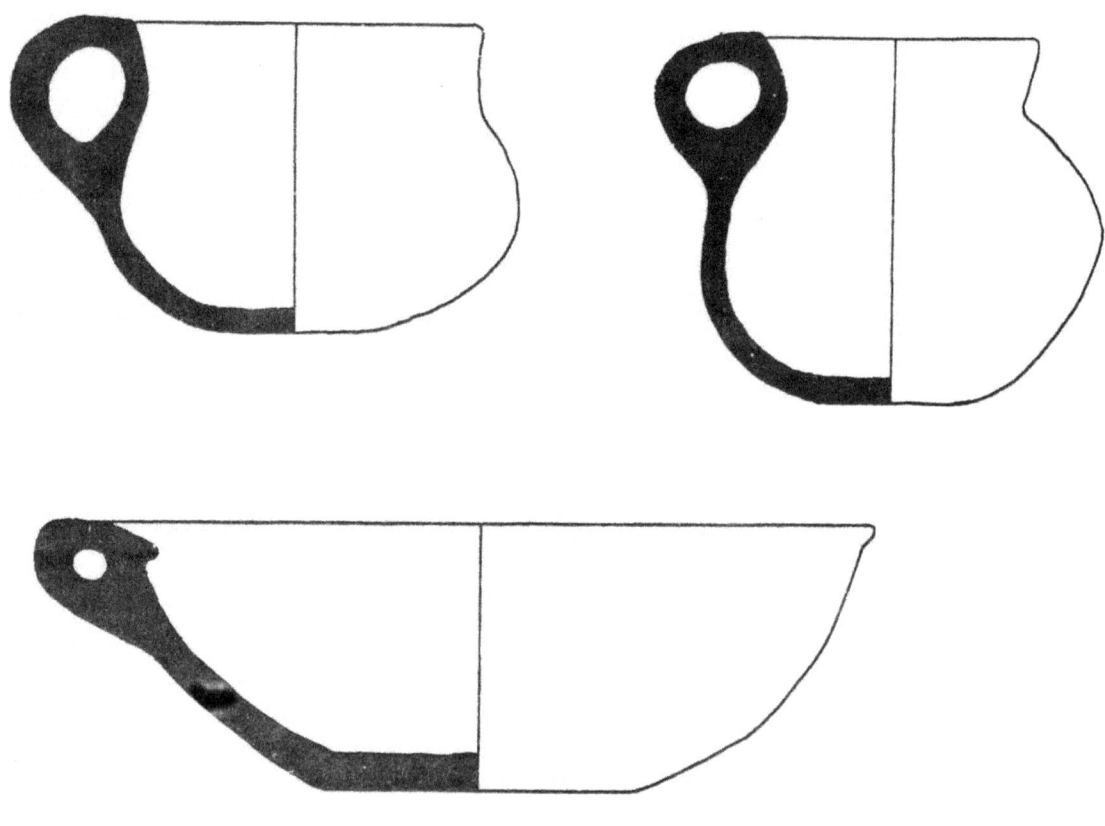

Fig. 3:2 Examples of Bell Beaker accompanying pottery from Bohemia. Scale 1:2.

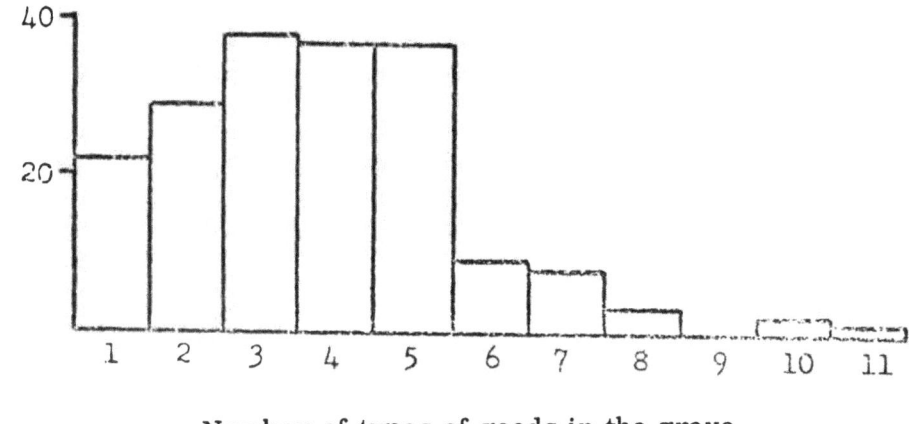

a

Number of types of goods in the grave

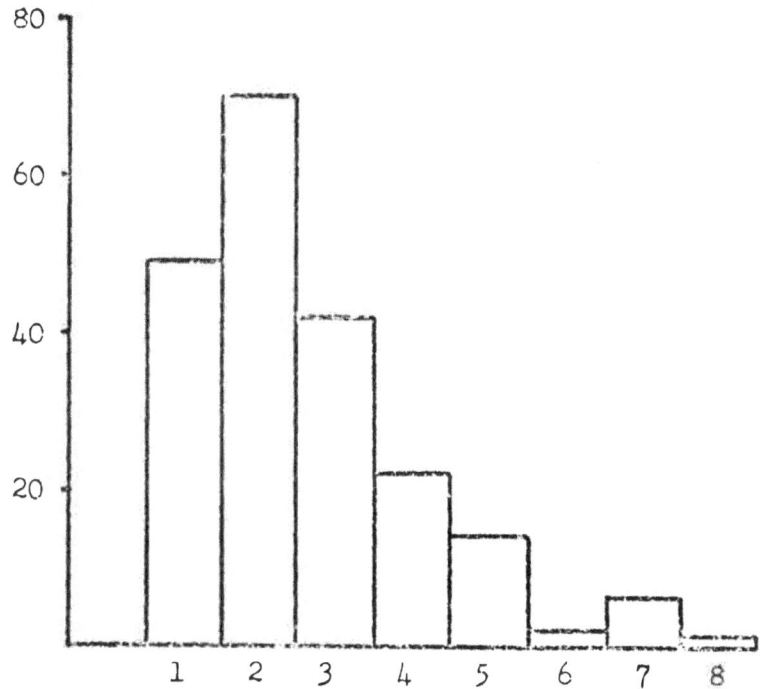

b

Number of types of goods in the grave

Fig. 3:3 Bar graph of number of graves against the number of types of goods in the grave. Comparison of Bohemian Corded Ware and Bohemian Bell Beakers. a) Corded Ware b) Bell Beakers.

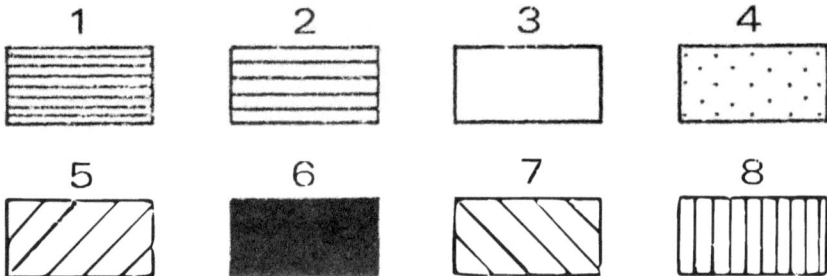

Key:
1. Chernozem
2. Brown soils
3. Podsolic soils and brown forest soils
4. Brown forest soils of mountains
5. Podsols of mountains
6. Grey forest soils
7. Rendzina soils
8. Soils of flood plain

Fig. 3:4   The distribution of Bell Beaker sites in Central Germany in relation to soil types.   Scale 1:2,000,000.

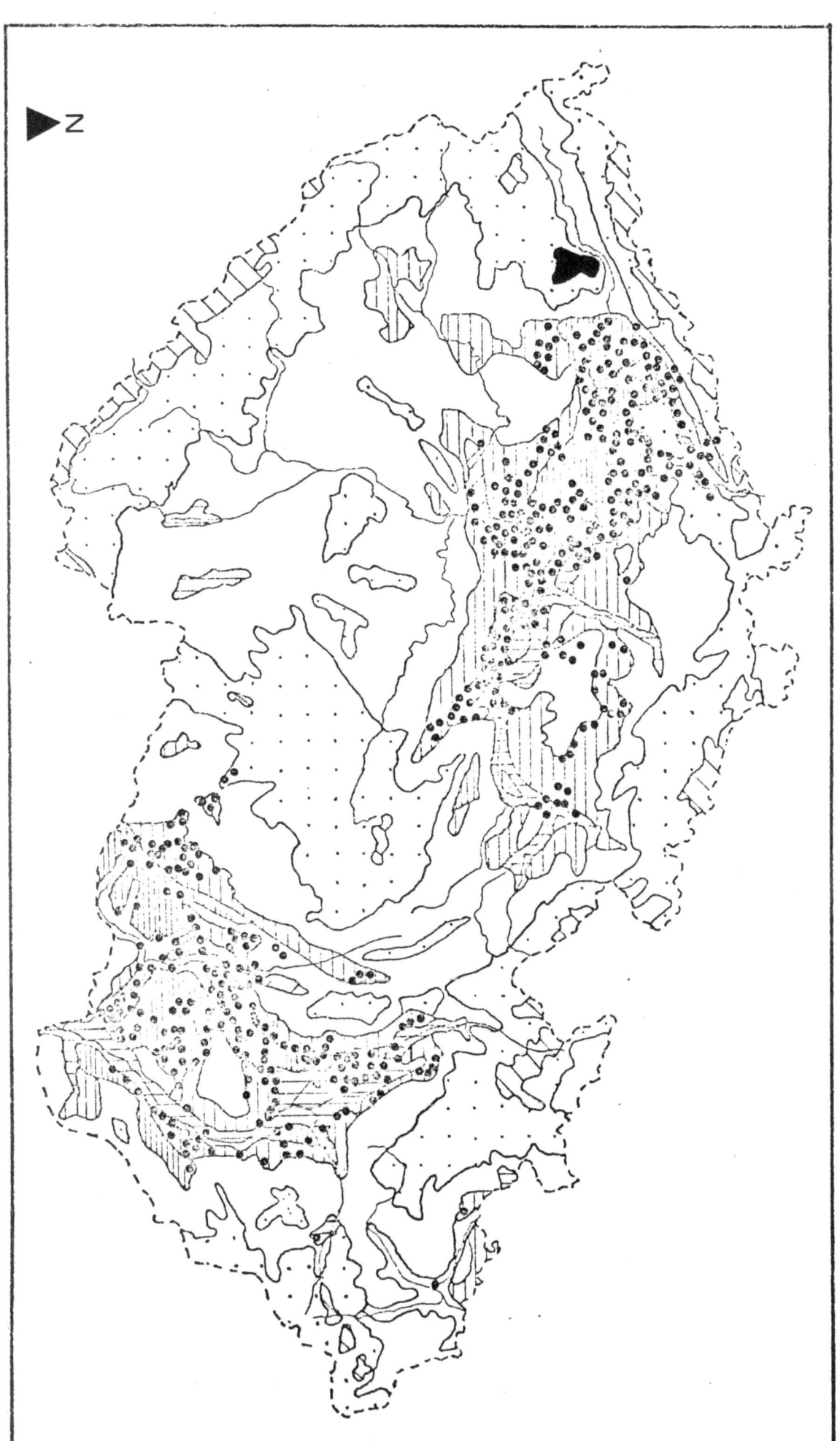

Fig. 3:4　The distribution of Bell Beaker sites in Bohemia and Moravia in relation to soil types.　Scale 1:2,000,000.

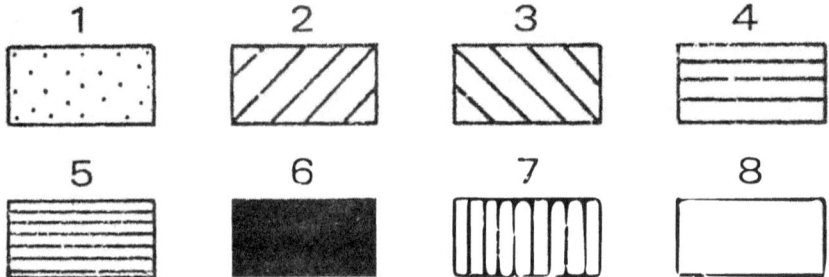

Key: 1. Black earth on loess
2. Black earth on detritus marl
3. Degraded black earth on loess
4. Forest soils on loess
5. Forest soils on silt and sand
6. Moorland soils
7. Rocky soils
8. Wet soils

Fig. 3:5 The distribution of Bell Beaker sites in Central Germany in relation to soil types. Scale 1:1,175,000.

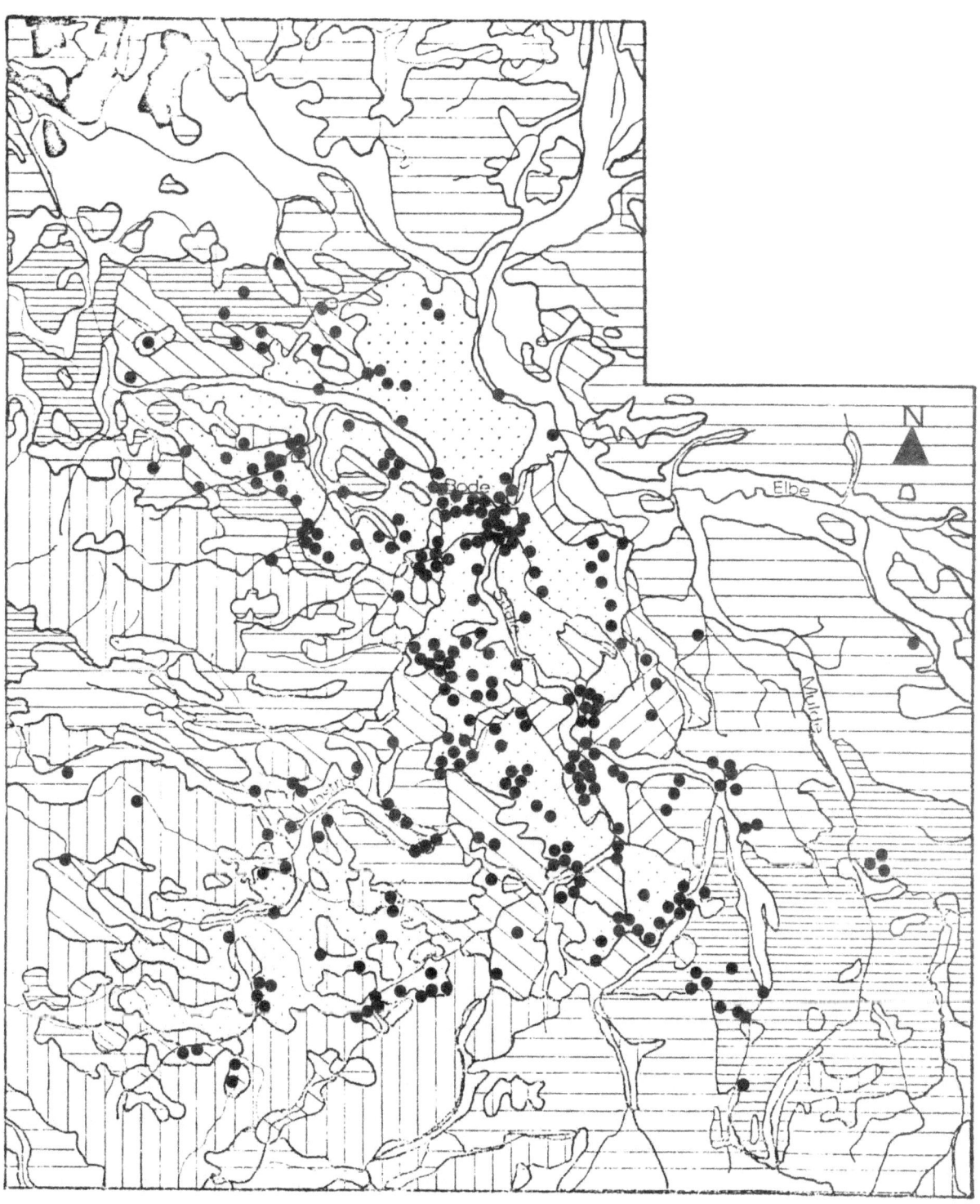

Central Germany	Bohemia	Moravia	Hungary
Bernburg	Řivnáč	Jevišovice B	
Earlier Corded Ware	Later Corded Ware	Later Corded Ware	Makó
Mansfeld Corded Ware/			
Bell Beakers	Bell Beakers	Bell Beakers	Bell Beaker- Csepel Group
Únětice	Únětice	Únětice	Nagyrév

Fig. 3:6   Chronological inter-relations of the Late Neolithic - Early Bronze Age cultures for the major Bell Beaker areas of Central Europe.

4. THE BEAKER CULTURE IN BRITAIN AND IRELAND

Humphrey Case

SUMMARY

The Beaker Culture in Britain and Ireland is best considered in three phases. An Early phase in which cord-impressed beakers were prominent was succeeded by the Middle phase, which sets the major pattern for Britain and Ireland. Unlike the Early phase, the Middle phase may have been initiated by settlers from the continent of Europe, but thereafter many of its features can be explained as brought about by exchanges between static communities, both within these islands and abroad. Mixed farming was pursued energetically; innovations included copper- and bronze-metallurgy and gold working. Settlement was dispersed, but society was probably organised hierarchically. The Late phase sees the insular persistence of the Beaker Culture after it had ceased on the continent. It is essentially a continuation of the Middle phase and its features may be explained by a similar pattern of exchanges.

DEFINITIONS, PHASES AND STYLES

Even following the strictest definition (Childe 1956) the existence of a pan-European Bell-Beaker Culture is undeniable: comprising pots of generally similar form with variously similar detailed traits, associated with variously similar artefacts of materials other than pottery, distributed within a limited span of time over large and well-definable regions of the continent - the beakers themselves indeed extending to North Africa. This limited span of time in Britain and Ireland falls partly within the Late Neolithic and partly within the Early Bronze Age.

Calibrated radiocarbon chronology gives a better estimate of its duration (Fig. 1), and by means of the conveniently summarised conversion tables of Clark (1975) and the quartile method of analysis recommended by Ottaway (1973) it can be divided into: a putative Early phase, dating from the start of the Late Neolithic, around the turn of the 4th and 3rd millennia B.C.: a Middle phase, also Late Neolithic, from somewhat before the mid 3rd millennium; and a Late phase, dating from the start of the Early Bronze Age at the end of the 3rd millennium. The suffix B.C. throughout this paper indicates calibrated chronology, in contrast to b c which refers to conventional radiocarbon chronology.

The Middle and Late phases, and to some degree the Early, are conformable to typology, stratification and association; their most prevalent and variable type-fossils are the beakers themselves or their sherds, which may be divided into the Early, Middle and Late styles most characteristic of their respective phases, by simplifying the converging classifications of Piggott (1963), Clarke (1970) and Lanting and Van der Waals (1972). Thus an <u>Early style</u> (comprising Piggott's Cord-Zoned and Clarke's All-Over-Corded, and part of Lanting's and Van der Waal's Step 1: Fig. 3, no. 1) seems clearly separated from a <u>Late style</u> (Piggott's Long-Necked, Clarke's N3, N4 and S series, and Lanting's and Van der Waal's steps 5, 6 and 7: Fig. 6), while a <u>Middle style</u> (Figs. 3, nos. 2, 8, 13, 18 and Fig. 4), comprising all the rest, seems to lie between them.

The Middle and Late styles are also parts of two major complexes of associations (Piggott 1963; Case 1966; Clarke 1970, Appendix 3), while the Early style has no distinctive associations.

Beaker Pottery Styles	Piggott (1963)	Clarke (1970)	Lanting & Van der Waals (1972)
EARLY	Cord-Zoned	AOC	Part of Step 1
MIDDLE	Bell Barrel Short-Necked	E, W/MR, N/MR N/NR, BW E.Ang., N1/D, N2	Part of Step 1 Steps 2, 3, 4
LATE	Long-Necked	N3, N4 S1, S2, S3 S4, SH	Steps 5, 6, 7

This classification may seem, at first sight, a regression to the innocence of Thurnam (1871) and Abercromby (1912). However in most contexts involving fragmentary archaeological material a simple overall classification is potentially the most informative, especially in view of the insufficiently recognised approximate values of radiocarbon dating; and it also seems appropriate to the nature of pottery itself (David & Hennig 1972, 27-8). Exceptionally however, the complex classifications come into their own in studying regional interactions (see below p. 9) and will no doubt be further refined, hopefully by by trace-element analysis among other means.

Finally, although each of the styles is likely to be the one most characteristic of its phase, it must be stressed that no exclusive correspondence is claimed. For example, Early style beakers persisted throughout the Middle phase and probably into the Late. Regional distributions suggest that both Clarke's W/MR and East Anglian styles continued into the Late phase and that S1 and even N3 (Fig. 4, no. 3) emerged during the Middle phase. Barbed wire decoration was also a feature of both the Middle and Late phases.

ORIGIN AND CONTINUITY

Abercromby in 1912 explained the origin and continuity of the Beaker Culture in Britain and Ireland by waves of invaders or immigrants from the European continent; he had many followers leading to the late David Clarke (1970), with his theory of complex ethnic struggles and upheavals. An opposed opinion was reformulated recently by Burgess on east European analogy (Burgess and Shennan 1976): that the Beaker Culture may have been a fashion (Burgess termed it a cult package) which spread among more or less static societies - in southern England for example presumably among natives mainly of Grooved Ware affiliations. A third viewpoint however deserves favour: that archaeological evidence is not of a kind to be decisive in this sort of problem for any period of pre- or protohistory. History and ethnography give plentiful examples of changes in material culture having been brought about respectively by immigration and fashion, or by these processes operating in conjunction. A frank admission of the uncertainties is therefore appropriate, even if it implies an approach that seems excessively cautious to some. A compromise solution is thus adopted here: some settlers from the European continent, but also much interchange between settled communities in these islands, and involving those on the continent of Europe. Similarly, archaeology is unable to pronounce clearly as to precisely the direction from which the putative settlers or fashion may have reached us. Most likely from within north-west Europe must be sufficient answer for the purposes of this contribution; the best resemblances to our material lie there and limitations on movement over long distances are as likely to have applied to the Late Neolithic as to the Early (Case 1969).

EARLY BEAKER PHASE: from around the turn of the 4th and 3rd millennia B.C.

Clarke (1970) and Lanting and Van der Waals (1972) argued the priority of Early style (AOC) beakers basically by extrapolation from Dutch radiocarbon dates (Lanting et al. 1973, Lanting and Van der Waals 1976). There is however internal support for their arguments, since the earliest dated beaker pottery in these islands is cord-impressed. Two rim sherds were emphatically associated by the excavator with the constructional phase of the Giants' Hills long barrow, Skendleby, Lincs (Phillips 1935) which has been dated to 2460 ± 150 b c, BM-191, 3190 B.C. and 2370 ± 150 b c, BM-192, 3055 + B.C. Although these dates are among the earliest Bell-beaker dates in Europe, older than those for Dutch All-Over-Ornamented beakers from which the beakers concerned might be assumed to have been derived, and almost as early as any dates for Corded Ware, they may nonetheless be taken as relatively correct. Cord-impressed sherds showing traits common both to Corded Ware and to AOC beakers are recurrent in Late Neolithic Sandhills Ware assemblages in Northern Ireland. Such an assemblage at Goodland, Antrim (Case 1973) has termini ante and post quem which embrace the Skendleby dates (2200 ± 200 b c, D-46, 2850 B.C.; 2625 ± 135 b c, UB-320E, 3400 B.C.). Some of the sherds at Goodland and elsewhere (for instance loc.cit. fig. 4, no. 10; fig. 8, no. 29) carry motifs of hatched pendant triangles of a kind which Childe long ago compared to those on Corded Ware (in Herring 1941, 46). One of these sherds from Goodland is of exceptional grog-filled fabric, akin to that of pottery of the Swedish Boat-Axe Culture (according to information kindly given by Mrs. Birgitta Hulthén, Lund); and other sherds there of similar fabric bear zonal motifs which would be at home on All-Over-Corded beakers (for example, loc.cit. fig. 7, no. 25).

If we may infer therefore that AOC beakers were the earliest in these islands, it would nonetheless be mistaken to assume that they belonged exclusively to an Early phase. Sherds at the radiocarbon-dated settlements of Newgrange, Meath (O'Kelly 1973) and Ballynagilly, Tyrone (ApSimon 1976) date from the start of the Middle phase, and the radiocarbon date for beakers of this style from Helmsley, Yorks (1800 ± 150 b c, BM-62, 2230 B.C.) is well within it. Radiocarbon dated contexts at the multi-period henge monument at Mount Pleasant, Dorset, suggest that such beakers survived into the Late phase (information on Mount Pleasant kindly given by Drs. I. H. Longworth and G. J. Wainwright). Cord-impressed ornament was certainly a feature of the Late style, for example at the wedge-shaped gallery grave, Ballyedmonduff, Dublin (Ó Ríordáin and de Valéra 1952). The few associations in graves, settlements and other contexts point the same way: the occasional barbed-and-tanged arrowhead is common to Middle style associations; the gold earring from Alston, Northumberland (Clarke 1970, Fig. 3) is similar to those in Middle style association at Radley, Berks (Fig. 3, nos. 3, 4) and the same type of ornament in copper or bronze is associated with Late style beakers at Buxton, Derbys (Clarke 1970, Fig. 910) and Tallington, Lincs (Simpson 1976), and occurs in the Early Bronze Age Migdale Hoard, Sutherland (Piggott and Mitchell 1958).

The evidence indicates therefore that the Early style persisted all through the duration of the Beaker Culture in these islands. How is one to explain its early occurrence? The lack of specific associations seems in favour of fashion - for example through exchange of ideas in the making of cord-impressed pottery, and perhaps the exchange of gifts, in seasonal movements early in the Late Neolithic, between native British and Irish communities and those of a north European branch of the great family of Corded Ware cultures. Possibly some All-Over-Corded (AOC) beakers found their way here, or were made here as a result of such exchanges.

Nothing gives definite grounds for suggesting an influx of settlers into Britain and Ireland in the Early phase. Coastal settlement-sites more or less exclusively with sherds of cord-impressd beakers or with many occur however in north Britain, for example at Ross Links, Northumberland and Tusculum, East Lothian, and may have been more widespread than they appear. The fact that they generally only survive north of the eustatic-isostatic tilt line may perhaps suggest that further south their sister sites have become submerged; they may all thus have been part of a related complex of settlements around the North Sea, such as that being excavated at Aartswoud in the western Netherlands from which radiocarbon dates at least as early as any in Britain and Ireland have been provisionally reported.

The conclusion then is that while on present evidence the beginning of the Beaker Culture in these islands seems explainable by fashion, the question is very open and is likely to remain so.

Whichever is the correct explanation, it is probably however generally assumed that fashion or settlers originated in the Lower Rhine Basin. This matter must also be regarded as somewhat undecided. Lanting and Van der Waals (1973 and 1976) have argued that AOO beakers (with which AOC may be grouped) were linked in the Lower Rhine Basin in a continuous development with PFB beakers which are part of the Corded Ware family. Fig. 6 appears to support this contention strongly, showing the inner quartile of AOO dates as it were totally embedded in that referable to PFB. Close relationships of AOO and PFB with Corded Ware or allied assemblages throughout Europe would also be consistent with their overlap with dates from South Scandinavia, central Europe and the Soviet Union (Fig. 2).

Unexpectedly however the Dutch dates appear to be the earliest of all, alike in medians and inner and outer quartiles, if only marginally. The anomaly is somewhat marked if one considers the dates from south Scandinavia which appear fairly coherent internally, since dates available for Under, Ground and Upper Graves (at best rather approximate terms chronologically but nonetheless those on which the Lanting and Van der Waals system leans heavily) fall generally into sequence, and those for the Late Neolithic follow on plausibly - with that for the Myrhøj settlement, Jutland (1910 ± 100 b c, K-2067, Jensen 1972) appearing appropriately transitional. In the view of Lanting and Van der Waals early PFB should be contemporary with the Under Graves and AOO with the Ground Graves, whereas in Fig. 6 they both appear to be earlier.

Statistically these inconsistencies are insignificant and may have methodological explanations, but they serve to draw attention to the fact that the chronological relationships which ultimately must form the basis for the conception of AOO beakers - the relationships between the various groups of what can loosely be termed the Corded Ware complex or can be related to it - are no nearer agreement than those between the various Bell-Beaker groups. In this rather uncertain state of affairs it is worth emphasising that pottery with impressions of twisted cords was pre-Corded Ware in north-west Europe. It appeared in the so-called Early Neolithic in south Scandinavia of the late 4th or early 3rd millennium bc. It was probably no later in southern England in the Decorated style; and in Britain and Ireland there was a consistent tradition of zonal impressions in the Middle Neolithic Peterborough and Sandhills Wares of the mid 3rd millennium b c, combined in the Late Neolithic as we have seen with fringes and chevrons. Typologically and on present chronological evidence it would thus be possible to infer a contribution to AOC beakers from Ireland or Britain, where as we have seen they were long-lasting. Time will show whether this possibility can be seriously maintained.

MIDDLE BEAKER PHASE: from somewhat before the mid 3rd millennium B.C. until its end

Arrival of settlers from the European mainland is assumed to have initiated the Middle phase. Their arrival may have been part of renewed movements in north-west Europe both of people and ideas, which cut short the making of All-Over-Corded beakers in the Netherlands and brought in there the series of Maritime - Locally Developed - Barbed Wire beakers, which some of the British and Irish Middle phase beakers closely resemble, and with which they were absolutely contemporary as Fig. 1 shows.

The argument for newcomers can be advanced not simply on account of the Middle phase Beaker Culture (with its associated economy, technology and ritual) appearing an innovation as seen against the Late Neolithic background, but through its being associated also with what has been claimed to be an intrusive robust and brachycephalic human skeletal type. This claim by Abercromby (1912), following among others Thurnham (1871), has been supported generally by physical anthropologists up to the present day, for example by Brothwell and Krzanowski (1974). Gerhardt (1976, 156-7) has noted apparent resemblances between British and continental Beaker Culture skulls. The survival in eastern England of the apparently strongly contrasting native gracile dolichocephalic type to the Early Beaker phase is seen at the Giants' Hills long barrow, Skendleby (Cave in Phillips 1935).

Late Neolithic physical anthropology could no doubt profitably be thoroughly reassessed, but until that is done there seems no reason not to accept traditional opinion that the Beaker Culture in Britain and Ireland was to some degree associated with an intrusive ethnic type.

The new settlers appear to have taken in land determinedly. Although appreciable clearances of forest are implied in the Middle Neolithic by monuments such as Newgrange, Meath or Meldon Bridge, Peebles (Burgess 1976) and by the Late Neolithic henge monuments in southern England, enduring and widespread clearances in Britain and Ireland on both good and marginal soils date from the Middle Beaker phase and continue into the Late. They are more impressive than the landnams of the Middle Neolithic, and repeatedly see the beginning of more or less irreversible phases of grassland and heaths. Many are unrelated to archaeological material, but there are associations both direct and by implication with the Beaker Culture (some examples in Evans 1972; others in northern Ireland, Smith 1975, and especially at Ballynagilly, ApSimon 1976). These clearances set the pattern for the ensuing Bronze Age, and can be seen as following a similar widespread surge of agrarian effort and clearance in the European continent recognisable for example in Little Poland, Switzerland and South Scandinavia in Corded Ware contexts, also in the Paris Basin and Brittany.

Users of Middle style beakers were exceptionally energetic mixed farmers. Cattle have been most frequently recorded among the livestock. Those at the Newgrange settlement were exceptionally large and the breed of pigs was among the largest in prehistoric Europe (Van Wijngaarden Bakker 1974). The longifrons breed of cattle may have been brought to Britain by beaker people (Jewell 1963) and the horse introduced to Ireland (Van Wijngaarden Bakker 1974). According to the present state of research, impressions of grains have been noted more often on beakers (of all styles) than on Early Bronze Age Food Vessels and Urns (Jessen and Helbaek 1944; Helbaek 1952); and none whatsoever have been detected on contemporary Grooved Ware or Peterborough Ware (although recent excavations at Skara Brae will no doubt give a fuller picture than previously obtained of an economy associated with Grooved Ware, even if from rather a specialised environment). Emmer, einkorn and bread wheat, barley including apparently 6 and 4 row variations, and flax were grown by beaker people. In contrast to the Middle Neolithic, barley has been the crop most frequently recorded, following a mainland European trend as seen in Corded Ware associations (Schultze-Motel 1969); but impressions of emmer wheat were slightly more numerous at Belle Tout, Sussex (Bradley 1970). Farming may be assumed to have been flexible and adaptable as in the Middle Neolithic (Dennell 1976), and a greater intake of marginal land (and possibly the deterioration of over-cultivated soils) may have favoured barley, any surplus of which will have been useful as fodder for livestock. Ploughing was recorded at the South Street Long Barrow near Avebury (Fowler and Evans 1967) and was possibly similarly dated at Barrow

G.71, Earl's Farm Down, near Amesbury, Wilts (Christie 1967). Cultivated fields were near the settlement at Belle Tout, Sussex (Bradley 1970). Hunting, fishing and gathering were not important activities, except on the coast.

Settlement traces associated with the Beaker Culture, some with many hundreds of sherds (Clarke 1970, and in Ireland especially Newgrange, O'Kelly 1973 and Ballynagilly, ApSimon 1976) are like grain impressions more numerous than those assignable to other Late Neolithic or Early Bronze Age cultures, adding to the impression of a widespread settled population. The estimate of population by Atkinson (1972) based on barrow burials is likely to be too low.

As in northern and central Europe generally, the pattern of settlement seems to have been dispersed, compatible with isolated or very small groups of farmsteads. The few house plans recorded (Bradley 1970; Simpson 1971) are of single-family or small extended-family size, including structures built on the surface and those partly dug into the subsoil, as elsewhere in north-west Europe at Molenaarsgraaf, western Netherlands (Louwe Kooijmans 1974) and Myrhøj, Jutland (Jensen 1972). Some settlement traces suggest seasonal occupation, for instance at Rockbarton, Limerick (Mitchell and Ó Ríordáin 1942) perhaps related there to a parent settlement nearby on Knockadoon (Ó Ríordáin 1954).

Seasonal activities may have included transhumance, flint-mining or collecting, and collecting and exchange of other rocks. These included foreign rocks (nephrite and perhaps Niedermendig lava) and rocks from widespread sources within Britain. Amber, jet and shale, for the occasional V-button (Fig. 4, nos. 7, 8, 10, 11), bead or belt-ring, were substances probably obtained in seasonal exchanges. Gold working and metallurgy seem explainable as other seasonal activities, and the balance of evidence indicates that users of the Middle beaker style of pottery introduced them to Britain and Ireland (Case 1966). The rather clumsily executed gold ear-rings and sundiscs (Fig. 3, nos. 3, 4, 9) do not suggest specialist craftsmen and the copper objects are of simple forms: tanged and rivet-tanged knives (Fig. 3, nos. 10, 14, 19, 20; Fig. 4, no. 5), double pointed awls of square section (Case 1966, Fig. 13, nos. 2-4), thick-butted axes (Case 1966 passim) and the occasional dress-pin (Clarke 1970, pl. 3). However the first lunulae should belong to this phase (note the degree of their similarity to Clarke's N2 beakers: Taylor 1970), and compared with the sundiscs and ear-rings their thicker metal and fine elegant tracing show a more extravagant and practised tradition of Irish gold working. Standardised copper-arsenical alloys (Coghlan and Case 1957), the occasional tin-bronze (Case 1965; Clarke 1970, 2, pl. 3) and sound castings show excellent competence. The extraction and production of copper and gold, and to some extent gold working, may thus have been part-time specialisations.

Knives of coppers comparable to these in Irish, German and Dutch contexts, suggest widespread exchanges, and English sundiscs may have been of Irish gold. In view of their association with the so-called impact phase of metallurgy, the earliest Irish halberds and thin-butted axes, based on central Rueopean models, also probably belonged to the Middle phase (Case 1966); as possibly did thin-butted axes in Scotland (Coles 1968/9).

So-called settlement pottery with impressed decoration (Clarke 1970) is recognisable from the Middle phase and plentiful for example at Newgrange and the Lough Gur sites. The beakers themselves show a tendency in Britain towards southern and northern variants: the southern (Fig. 3, nos. 2, 8, 13, 18) with bell-shaped or angular profiles and sweeping necks and with zonal decoration; the northern (Fig. 4) with straight or cupped necks and rather less emphatically zonal decoration, especially of fringes and zig-zags; both variants occasionally have panels (Fig. 4, nos. 9, 12) somewhat in the style of the central European Metopenbecher. Both the great regional variety and the evolution of Middle style pottery have been demonstrated and inferred by Clarke (1970) and by Lanting and Van der Waals (1972). Variety and evolution have often been explained following Abercromby (1912) by repeated immigrations with wave after wave of settlers, and by much shifting of ground within these islands. These explanations have been consistent with a view generally held throughout Europe that users of beakers were exceptionally nomadic, rapidly and often on the move, a view which seemed confirmed by conventional radiocarbon chronology giving rather a hectic speed to the Beaker Culture in Europe generally, by confining its major developments to only a few centuries. Use of a calibrated scale shows however that the Middle phase lasted about half a millennium in Britain and Ireland (Fig. 1); and there, as we have seen, Beaker Culture settlers seem unlikely to have been true nomads, wandering prospectors or specialist metallurgusts, but more or less static mixed-farmers like innumerable other European Late Neolithic populations. Thus once the Beaker Culture became effectively established in these islands in the Middle phase, it is as likely as not that variety and change in pottery and other artefacts were brought about by the development of regional traditions, as in the Middle Neolithic, and through comparatively peaceful interchanges between scattered communities, rather than by warfare or by political groupings.

Interchanges were made too with communities with long-standing native traditions. Burgess has indicated shared burial ritual (1976). Various associations have been noted of beaker pottery with other Late Neolithic wares: an important instance was in the filling of the lateral chambers of the West Kennet Long Barrow (Piggott 1962), where Middle style pottery occurred with Peterborough Ware (with the Fengate style dominant and a little Grooved Ware). Here beaker-using people may have pulled off the capstones during rebuilding of the Avebury henge-monument complex, and partly replaced them after filling the chambers with rubble and soil which contained much contemporary settlement-material (Case 1961). Such interference with earlier monuments was a widespread practice of beaker-using people, seen for example at Petit-Chasseur, Valais (Gallay 1976), Switzerland, and at Le Goërem, Gavres, Morbihan (L'Helgouach 1976), and in northern and southern Irish wedge-shaped gallery-graves and probably many Iberian monuments.

Beaker Culture flint industries are too little known at present, but they also appear to show some contact with other Late Neolithic cultures. This is discernible for instance in the industry at Belle Tout (Bradley 1970) and in the so-called "points" at Newgrange which resemble the transverse-derived arrow heads of southern English Grooved Ware sites (O'Kelly 1973). Note also an arrow-head of this type in the Late Beaker grave at Durrington G.67, Wilts (Fig. 6, no. 20).

The occurrence of gracile dolichocephalic skeletons (apparently resembling those of the Windmill Hill Culture) in Late and Middle phase graves (for instance at the Thickthorn Long Barrow, Dorset: Tydesley in Drew and Piggott 1936) may conceivably represent exchanges of kin with native populations.

Although beaker-using communities like many other societies may have indulged in parades of aggression, which some of the richer graves (Fig. 3, nos. 3-21; Fig. 4, nos. 4-8) may suggest (Piggott 1973) and in feuding and seasonal raiding, the role of warfare has probably been exaggerated. Offensive weapons seem confined to arrowheads, which are rare in graves (see below pp. 81-82) and not very frequent in settlements. Energy was expended on ritual works (see below, p. 80) and those connected with farming or settlement, for example the enclosure at Belle Tout (Bradley 1970) and the terracing at Site D, Lough Gur (Ó Ríordáin 1954), but not on fortification. Alternative explanations to warfare or political upheaval seem preferable for the definite but curiously diffuse and interpenetrated regional groups of pottery defined by Clarke in his fine series of distribution studies (1970): for example, exogamy (if pottery making was a woman's craft), emulation, exchanges and gifts, or even the work of specialist potters (Clarke 1976). Diffusion of traits could have been widespread in these ways through manifold contacts in Britain and Ireland, and further afield if settlers remained in touch with kin in ancestral areas of north-west Europe.

Such contacts could have been maintained by isolated farmers at seasonal gatherings, which would have provided the necessary foci not only for kinship arrangements but also for corporate identity and the settlement of disputes, and for mystery rites to influence an unpredictable environment. These gatherings will have been <u>interaction spheres</u> in Caldwell's definition (1964). Major centres for them may have been the stone circles and in southern England the great henge monuments - monuments of native Late Neolithic traditions in which users of beakers played varying, sometimes prominent roles and which required the assembly of large numbers of people to construct. Users of Middle style beakers were skilled stonemasons, as at Chatton Sandyford, Northumberland (Fig. 4, nos. 9-12. Jobey 1968), and the most prodigious achievement with which they are generally associated, in this direction, was the building of the double bluestone circle at Stonehenge, Wilts as part of the remodelling of the monument involving a change in its alignment (Stage II: Atkinson 1956). This endows users of Middle style beakers with remarkable engineering and astronomical ability.

Startin has recently calculated (1976) that a minimum of 70 able-bodied men would have been required for the major tasks associated with the Stage II monument. Many kinship groups would thus appear to have been involved, originating perhaps from a wide area of southern Britain - which is self-evident bearing in mind the likely Pembrokeshire origin of the bluestones themselves. This minimum number of able-bodied men would have been about the same as that required for the outer ring of the Windmill Hill causewayed camp, but the labour-input (some 250,000 man-hours) would have been more than 5 times as great, or (to express it another way) possibly more than 12 times that required for the subsistence agriculture needed to support the entire communities represented by the men concerned. Plainly the project was spread over a number of years.

THE TRANSITION BETWEEN THE MIDDLE AND LATE PHASES: end of the 3rd millennium B.C.

The most massive reconstruction at Stonehenge, involving the sarsen circle and trilithons (Stage III) must be taken on present evidence as little later than Stage II, and its inception at least can also thus be associated with the Beaker Culture (but compare Atkinson 1956 and Piggott 1973 for other interpretations). The radiocarbon dates assignable to the two stages are inseparable statistically: Stage II, 1620 ± 110 b c, I-2384, 2000 B.C.; Stage III, 1720 ± 150 b c, BM-46, 2120 B.C. (Such tiresome but minor stratigraphical inversions are not unusual in series of radiocarbon dates.) One recent date for the Avenue ditch at a point near the monument, generally held to be associated with Stage II, is consistent (1728 ± 68 b c, BM-1164, 2140 B.C., Atkinson and Vatcher 1976).

Rebuilding in sarsen at the henge-monument complex at Mount Pleasant, Dorset was contemporary (1680 ± 60 b c, BM-668, 2070 B.C.), but associated with Late as well as Middle style sherds. These four radiocarbon dates lie at the transition to the Late phase (where the inner quartiles of the two left hand diagrams of Fig. 1 would meet). This transitional period (termed Stage 3 in Case 1976) was thus one of great activity; and rebuilding at Avebury, Wilts., both perhaps within the monument itself and at the nearby Sanctuary and the joining of the two by the Kennet Avenue, may have been more or less contemporary and associated throughout with Middle style pottery. The transitional period may have been characterised by varying material culture and some of the richer graves of both Middle phase (Figs. 3 and 4) and Late phase associations (Fig. 6) may have lain within it.

Startin has calculated (1976) that about one and a half million man-hours would have been required for the tasks associated with the Stage III monument at Stonehenge, and that on occasions a minimum of some 600 able-bodied men would have been needed to haul the sarsens. The dressing of the sarsens would alone have required around half a million man-hours, and may thus have been spread over many years. This most time-consuming repetitive task may according to Startin indicate a slave class, in the sense of a group without land or cultivation- or grazing-rights, which could have been applied to it more or less uninterruptedly.

I evoke thus a picture of Beaker Culture society somewhat akin to that described for the Viking period in the Icelandic sagas: in the small dispersed settlements of mixed farmers, the existence of slaves in the sense suggested above, the pattern of exchanges (and of raids and feuds), and the far-flung connections and seasonal gatherings. Such may have been the social pattern in Britain and Ireland and over much of western Europe from the mid 3rd millennium B.C. until the Roman Conquest or later. In social organisation as well as in various skills the Middle phase may thus be seen as one of the more formative periods in British prehistory - even though a hierarchical form of society may have existed independently from the start of the Late Neolithic (Renfrew 1973) in Britain and Ireland, as monuments such as Meldon Bridge (Burgess 1976), the largest passage graves, or the great southern English henge monuments associated with Grooved Ware would seem to indicate.

Rich and poor Beaker Culture graves

Something of the social organisation of those who used beakers can also perhaps be inferred from their graves, although conceptions of richness and poverty may be wide of the mark in view of the fact that possibly only a narrow range of grave-goods survives. However for the purposes of argument, a comparatively rich burial is defined here as one containing a greater variety of goods.

As the record stands, by no means all burials were accompanied by any grave-goods; this can be seen for example at the Late phase Cassington and Eynsham cemeteries (Fig. 5) and may have been true of the majority of burials of both phases. Of those with grave-goods, a beaker alone was the most frequent association, then a beaker with another; other associations additional to a single beaker vary somewhat and as to the age and sex of the burial.

Age- and sex-determination are far from comprehensive or perhaps reliable, but according to the evidence as it exists: children's graves were the most poorly furnished, then women's, then men's. Flint flakes were on the whole the most frequent additional associations with children; and another beaker with women - a bronze awl being also a characteristically feminine association (for instance, Cassington cemetery grave 10, Eynsham grave 18: Fig. 5). Men were variously furnished, and the majority probably poorly, like women and children. The burial of women and children to some extent apart from men is noteworthy at the Late phase Cassington and Eynsham cemeteries (Fig. 5). (These cemeteries also illustrate the fact that the data available in Britain do not permit any hard-and-fast attribution of grave-orientation or position of the body to men or women or to a particular phase. Britain appears to differ in this respect from parts of the continent of Europe).

In both phases, some outstanding groups of burials with overlapping associations can be recognised more or less throughout Britain:

(1) Artisans' burials, with associations such as flint axes, antler picks or tines (Fig. 6, no. 14), or hammerstones of various kinds (Fig. 6, no. 17) are infrequent but occasionally quite rich (as for example the Late phase burial, Fig. 6, nos. 15-17 and one from the recently excavated Barrow 1, Site 2, Aldwincle, Northants, Jackson 1976) and are sometimes of women. The associations suggest that flint-knapping and perhaps digging may have been of lower status than metal-working.

(2) Arrowhead burials are rather infrequent. Never of women or children, they show no overlap with Artisans' burials, were predominantly southern English and slightly more numerous in the Middle phase; with some exceptions (as Fig. 4, nos. 2-7, 13-17; Fig. 6, nos. 18-20), they were generally poorly furnished. They may indicate the general status of feuding in Beaker Culture society: hunting seems generally to have figured little in the food-quest.

(3) Exceptionally rich burials are few and may perhaps be assumed to be of those of high status; where determinable, they were almost invariably of men. In the Middle phase, the most prominent group clusters around the

stone bracer or wristguard, which is the most frequent additional association with arrowheads; these graves have a southern English tendency (Fig. 3, nos. 8-12, 13-17, 18-21; cp. Fig. 4, nos. 4-8). A recently published example from the Midlands is from Barnack, Northants (Kinnes 1976).

While recognising the degree of unverifiable guessing involved (Ucko 1969/70, esp. 266-8, but cp. Shennan 1975), one can note the possible parallels between this apparently hierarchical pattern of men's burials and the social system described in the Icelandic sagas for the Viking period and in Indo-European tradition generally. The exceptionally rich burials might thus be seen as of those with major rights in land, being the kin of chiefs or wise men in Kehoe's sense (1974); the Arrowhead graves generally of those with lesser status but with rights as warriors; and the remaining furnished burials of those for the most part of lower status still; and some at least of the Artisan burials may have been of a landless or slave class, few of which may perhaps have been entitled to burial.

LATE BEAKER PHASE: from the end of the 3rd millennium B.C.

The Late phase, more or less contemporary with the south Scandinavian Late Neolithic (cp. Figs. 1 and 2), sees the insular persistence of the Beaker Culture after it had ended on the European mainland. Any major contribution by new settlers seems most unlikely.

In economy and settlement it is a continuation of the Middle. The oval house at Northton, Harris, off the north-west coast of Scotland, with two occupation levels (Simpson 1976), is however noteworthy as are numerous settlement traces suggesting seasonal occupation in the Fenlands of eastern England. In addition to the rebuilding of Mount Plesant, much other activity at the henge monuments was associated with the Late style: construction of the Grange Circle, Limerick (Ó Ríordáin 1951), activity at Durrington Walls and construction or major activity at Gorsey Bigbury, Somerset (ApSimon et al. 1976), and at the Big Rings, Dorchester, Oxon. (from information kindly given by Mr. N. Thomas). Burial ritual continued the earlier Neolithic traditions seen in the Middle phase: under round barrows, within ring-ditches, as secondaries in long barrows and megaliths, in stone cists and as groups of graves unprotected by prominent earthworks. Cremation became a little more common. Cemeteries of rather less than 20 burials were recorded at Cassington and Eynsham, Oxfordshire, in the Upper Thames Valley (Fig. 5) and at Staxton in the East Riding of Yorkshire; similar clusters have been quite often found in and under barrows in the East Riding and for instance, the Peak District (Petersen 1972). The robust brachycephalic skeletal type was apparently in evidence in the Oxfordshire cemeteries and its survival for possibly a millennium may perhaps indicate the effectiveness of kinship-arrangements.

The material culture too shows a massive continuation from the Middle phase. Similar settlement pottery was used. The cupped and chimney-like necks and broken and panelled motifs of Late style beakers (Fig. 6) all have their roots in the Middle style, especially in north Britain. Specific features of the Middle style surviving alongside the Late can be seen at the Northton settlement, Harris (Simpson 1976) and the Cassington cemetery, Oxon.

Various associations show continuity from types current in the Middle phase or which may in some cases have originated at the transitional period (see above, p. 80 ; Case 1976): they comprise V-buttons (Fig. 6, nos. 4, 9, 10; cp. Fig. 4, nos. 7, 8, 10, 11), belt-rings (Fig. 6, no. 5), bone, antler and stone spatulae (Fig. 6, nos. 2, 3; cp. Fig. 3, no. 11), bone points (for instance, Clarke 1970, Figs. 663, 776), flint daggers (Fig. 6, nos. 11, 16), tin-bronzes, thin butted and flanged axes - and perhaps decorated examples (of Killaha and Ballyvalley types; Harbison 1969), and lunulae and probably halberds.

Some innovations appear: for example awls with rounded sections and a chisel-end (Annable and Simpson 1964, 90, no. 78), and a bronze razor (Clarke 1970, Fig. 1013). Some indicate continuing contacts with the European mainland: stone shaft-hole axe-hammers (Fig. 6, no. 19) lasted there from Corded Ware times through the duration of the Middle phase in Britain (Lanting 1973); the so-called cushion stones (Fig. 6, no. 17) also have continental parallels (Butler and Van der Waals 1966). Handled beakers may show the influence of continental Early Bronze Age wares, and copper or bronze ornaments including beads (Fig. 6, nos. 24-6), bracelets or arm-rings (Clarke 1970, Figs. 674, 955) follow central European fashions.

Bronze riveted knives or daggers (Fig. 6, no. 22), and flint arrow heads with long square-cut tangs (Piggott 1963; Clarke 1970, fig. 892) do not have very specific continental parallels. Similarly, contemporary graves without beakers but containing bronze daggers associated with thin-butted axes (Gerloff 1975, Pl. 42), show a combination which was extremely widespread in the Early Bronze Age of central and western Europe. All these changes are best seen as the result of continuing interplay of techniques and ideas in seasonal movements between otherwise fairly settled mixed-farming populations.

Poorly furnished burials, Artisans', Arrowhead and exceptionally rich burials can all be recognised in the Late phase. Three overlapping groups of exceptionally rich burials with regional variations are associated with bone, or stone spatulae (Fig. 6, nos. 2-3); with fire-making equipment (iron ore and flint strike-a-lights: Fig. 6, no. 8); and with shale or jet buttons (nos. 4, 9, 10) and belt-rings (no. 5). The relatively pacific nature of these associations may suggest that high status, at any rate in the Late phase, did not necessarily reside in political power as conventionally understood, as Kehoe has suggested (1974).

Burials with more unusual associations, tend to be marginal to the above-defined groups or even lacking in other associations than a beaker: this is true to some extent of flint daggers (Fig. 6, nos. 11, 16), more so of stone axe-hammers (Fig. 6, no. 19) and definitely so of riveted daggers (no. 22) and bronze ornaments. Indeed ornaments, except for gold embellishments in the Middle phase and belt-rings and buttons in both phases, are not generally associated with exceptionally rich graves as defined here.

Relationships with other Cultures

The replacement of the Beaker Culture by the Food Vessel and Urn complexes, which partly continued its traditions, can also be explained as part of a process of exchanges of techniques and ideas rather than by warlike or political upheaval. Food Vessels were contemporary with Late beakers (Fig. 1), but tended to supersede them stratigraphically. Some aspects of Food Vessels can be traced to Middle style beakers, for example, false-relief as at Ballynagilly (ApSimon 1976), but claims can be made that other Late or even Middle Neolithic pottery contributed to their origins (Manby 1975; Burgess 1976). Various kinds of Urn may also have had similarly early roots (Fig. 1), and partly in Beaker Culture settlement pottery; but their main development was at the end of the Late Beaker phase and they tended to supersede both beakers and Food Vessels. Food Vessels and Urns are often assumed to represent acculturation of long-standing native Late Neolithic populations by Beaker Culture innovators.

Finally, it should be noted that relationships with the Wessex Culture seem marginal or generalised (as seen for instance in bone pommels such as Fig. 6, no. 23); the few radiocarbon dates available from that culture suggest that it was successive to the Late phase but overlapped with it, and that its inner quartile on such a diagram as Fig. 1 may eventually be seen to lie between 1600 and 1275 b c. Construction and rebuilding at Stonehenge is likely to have continued well into this time span; this is likely enough both in view of the very laborious tasks involved (see above p. 80) and of a radiocarbon determination (1240 ± 105 b c, I-2445, 1539 B.C.) from the filling of Y-hole 30 (Atkinson 1956, late Stage III). For the building and modification of the major part of Stonehenge to have extended possibly over six centuries is by no means inconceivable on analogy with cathedrals or major parish churches.

BIBLIOGRAPHY

References not given in the text should be consulted in Piggott 1963, Case 1966 and D.L. Clarke 1970.

Abercromby, J., 1912.   Bronze Age Pottery, I.

Annable, F.K. and D.D.A. Simpson, 1964.   Guide Catalogue of the Neolithic and Bronze Age Collections in Devizes Museum.

ApSimon, A.M., 1976.   "Ballynagilly and the beginning and end of the Irish Neolithic", Acculturation and Continuity in Atlantic Europe, (ed. S.J. de Laet), 15-30.

ApSimon, A.M., Musgrave, J.H., Sheldon, J., Tratman, E.K., and Van Wijngaarden-Bakker, L.H., 1976.   "Gorsey Bigbury, Cheddar, Somerset", Proceedings University of Bristol Spelaeological Society 14, 155-83.

Atkinson, R.J.C., 1956.   Stonehenge.

Atkinson, R.J.C., 1972.   "Burial and Population in the British Bronze Age" in Prehistoric Man in Wales and the West: essays in honour of Lily F. Chitty (ed. F. Lynch and C. Burgess), 107-16.

Atkinson, R.J.C. and Vatcher, F. & L., 1976.   "Radiocarbon dates for the Stonehenge Avenue", Antiquity 50, 239-40.

Bradley, R., 1970.   "The excavation of a Beaker settlement at Belle Tout, East Sussex, England", Proceedings of the Prehistoric Society 36, 312-79.

Brothwell, D. and Krzanowski, W., 1974.   "Evidence of biological differences between British populations from Neolithic to Medieval times, as revealed by eleven commonly available cranial vault measurements", Journal of Archaeological Science 1, 249-60.

Burgess, C., 1976.   "Meldon Bridge: a Neolithic defended promontory complex near Pebbles" in Settlement and Economy in the Third and Second Millennia B.C., ed. C. Burgess & R. Miket (British Archaeological Reports 33), 151-79.

Burgess, C. and Shennan, S., 1976.   "The Beaker phenomenon: some suggestions" in Settlement and Economy in the Third and Second Millennia B.C., ed. C. Burgess & R. Miket (British Archaeological Reports 33) 309-31.

Butler, J.J. and van der Waals, J.D., 1966.   "Bell-beakers and early metal-working in the Netherlands", in Neolithic Studies in Atlantic Europe (ed. J.D. van der Waals) Palaeohistoria 12, 41-139.

Caldwell, J.R., 1964. "Interaction spheres in prehistory", Hopewellian studies: Scientific papers (ed. J.R. Caldwell & R.L. Hall), 12 (6), 133-43.

Case, H.J., 1961. Review of S. Piggott, The West Kennet Long Barrow. Archaeological Journal 118, 253-4.

Case, H.J., 1965. "A tin-bronze in Bell-Beaker association", Antiquity 39, 219-22.

Case, H.J., 1966. "Were Beaker-people the first metallurgists in Ireland?", in Neolithic Studies in Atlantic Europe (ed. J.D. van der Waals), Palaeohistoria 12, 141-77.

Case, H.J., 1969. "Neolithic explanations", Antiquity 43, 176-86.

Case, H.J., 1973. "A Ritual Site in North-East Ireland" in Megalithic Graves and Ritual, (ed. G. Daniel & P. Kjaerum),173-96.

Case H.J., 1976. "Contextual archaeology and the Beaker Culture", in Glockenbecher Symposion: Oberried 1974, (ed. J.N. Lanting & J.D. van der Waals),453-8.

Childe, V.G., 1956. Piecing Together the Past: the Interpretation of Archaeological Data.

Christie, P.M., 1967. "A Barrow-Cemetery of the Second Millenium B.C. in Wiltshire, England", Proceedings of the Prehistoric Society 33, 336-66.

Clark, R.M., 1975. "A calibration curve for radiocarbon dates", Antiquity 49, 251-66.

Clarke, D.L., 1970. Beaker Pottery of Great Britain and Ireland 1, 2.

Clarke, D.L., 1976. "The Beaker network - social and economic models", in Glockenbecher Symposion: Oberried 1974, (ed. J.N. Lanting & J.D. van der Waals),459-70.

Coghlan, H.H. and Case, H.J., 1957. "Early metallurgy of Copper in Ireland and Britain", Proceedings of the Prehistoric Society 23, 91-123.

Coles, J.M., 1968/9. "Scottish Early Bronze Age Metalwork", Proceedings of the Society of Antiquaries of Scotland 101, 1-110.

David, N. and Henning, H., 1972. "The Ethnography of Pottery: a Fulani Case Seen in Archaeological Perspective", Addison-Wesley Modular Publications 21, 1-29.

Dennell, R.W., 1976. "Prehistoric crop cultivation in southern England: a reconsideration", Antiquaries Journal 56, 11-23.

Drew, C.D. and Piggott, S., 1936. "The Excavation of Long Barrow 163a on Thickthorn Down, Dorset", Proceedings of the Prehistoric Society 2, 77-96.

Evans, J.G., 1972. Land Snails in Archaeology.

Fowler, P.J., and Evans, J.G., 1967. "Plough-Marks, Lynchets and Early Fields", Antiquity 41, 289-301.

Gallay, A., 1976. "The position of the Bell-Beaker Civilisation in the chronological sequence of Petit-Chasseur (Sion, Valais, Switzerland)" in Glockenbecher Symposion: Oberried 1974, (ed. J.N. Lanting and J.D. van der Waals), 271-306.

Gerhardt, K., 1976. "Anthropotypologie der Glockenbecherleute in ihren Ausschwärmelandschaften" in Glockenbecher Symposion: Oberried 1974, (ed. J. N. Lanting & J. D. van der Waals), 147-64.

Gerloff, S., 1975. The Early Bronze Age Daggers in Great Britain: Prähistorische Bronzefunde. Abteilung VI, 2. Band.

Harbison, P., 1969. The Axes of the Early Bronze Age in Ireland: Prähistorische Bronzefunde. Abteilung IX, 1. Band.

Helbaek, H., 1952. "Early Crops in Southern England", Proceedings of the Prehistoric Society 18, 194-233.

Herring, I., 1941. "The Tammyrankin Cairn: West Structure", Journal of the Royal Society of Antiquaries of Ireland 71, 31-52.

Jackson, D.A., 1976. "The Excavation of Neolithic and Bronze Age Sites at Aldwincle, Northants, 1967-71", Northamptonshire Archaeology 2, 12-70.

Jensen, J.A., 1972. "Myrhøj, 3 hustomter med klokkebaegerkeramik", Kuml 1972, 61-122 (English summary, 114-21).

Jessen, K. and Helbaek, H., 1944. Cereals in Great Britain and Ireland in prehistoric and early historic times.

Jewell, P., 1963. "Cattle from British archaeological sites", in Man and Cattle, ed. A.E. Mourant and F.E. Zeuner, 80-101.

Jobey, G., 1968. "Excavations of cairns at Chatton Sandyford, Northumberland", Archaeologia Aeliana 4S, 46, 5-50.

Kehoe, A.B., 1974. "Saints of Wessex?", Antiquity 48, 232-3.

Kinnes, I., 1976. "The Barnack Grave-Group", Dunobrivae 4, 16-17.

Lanting, J.N., 1973. "Laat-Neolithicum en Vroege Bronstijd in Nederland en N.W.-Duitsland: continue ontwikkelingen", Palaeohistoria 15, 216-317 (German summary 313-7).

Lanting, J.N. and van der Waals, J.D., 1972. "British Beakers as seen from the Continent", Helinium 12, 20-46.

Lanting, J.N., Mook, W.G. and van der Waals, J.D., 1973. "C^{14} chronology and the Beaker problem", Helinium 13, 38-58.

Lanting, J.N., and van der Waals, J.D., 1976. "Beaker Culture Relations in the Lower Rhine Basin", in Glockenbecher Symposion: Oberried 1974, (ed. J.N. Lanting & J.D. van der Waals), 1-80.

L'Helgouach, J., 1976. "Les relations entre le groupe des vases campaniformes et les groupes néolithiques dans l'Ouest de la France", in Glockenbecher Symposion: Oberried 1974, (ed. J.N. Lanting & J.D. van der Waals), 439-452.

Longworth, I.H., 1961. "The Origins and Development of the Primary Series in the Collared Urn Tradition in England and Wales", Proceedings of the Prehistoric Society 27, 263-306.

Louwe Kooijmans, L.P., 1974. The Rhine/Meuse Delta.

Manby, T., 1975. "Neolithic occupation sites on the Yorkshire Wolds", Yorkshire Archaeological Journal 47, 23-59.

Mitchell, G.F., and Ó Ríordáin, S.P., 1942. "Early Bronze Age Pottery from Rockbarton Bog, Co. Limerick", Proceedings of the Royal Irish Academy 48, C, 255-72.

O'Kelly, M.J., 1973. "Current excavations at Newgrange, Ireland", in Megalithic Graves and Ritual, (ed. G. Daniel and P. Kjaerum), 137-46.

Ó Ríordáin, S.P., 1951. "Lough Gur Excavations: the Great Stone Circle (B) in Grange Townland", Proceedings of the Royal Irish Academy 54, C, 37-74.

Ó Ríordáin, S.P., 1954. "Lough Gur Excavations: Neolithic and Bronze Age houses on Knockadoon", Proceedings of the Royal Irish Academy 56, C, 297-459.

Ó Ríordáin, S.P. and R. de Valéra, 1952. "Excavation of a Megalithic Tomb at Ballyedmonduff, Co. Dublin", Proceedings of the Royal Irish Academy 55, C, 61-81.

Ottaway, B., 1973. "Dispersion diagrams: a new approach to the display of carbon-14 dates", Archaeometry 15, 5-12.

Petersen, F., 1972. "Traditions of multiple burial in Later Neolithic and Early Bronze Age Britain", Archaeological Journal 129, 22-55.

Phillips, C.W., 1935. "The Excavation of the Giants' Hills Long Barrow, Skendleby, Lincolnshire", Archaeologia 85 (1936), 37-106.

Piggott, S., 1962. The West Kennet Long Barrow.

Piggott, S., 1963. "Abercromby and after: the Beaker Cultures of Britain re-examined", in Culture and Environment (ed. I. Ll. Foster & L. Alcock), 53-91.

Piggott, S., 1973. "The later Neolithic: Single Graves and the first metallurgy", in A History of Wiltshire, ed. E. Crittall, I part 2, 333-51 (The Victoria History of the Counties of England, ed. R.B. Pugh).

Renfrew, C., 1973. "Monuments, mobilisation and social organisation in neolithic Wessex", in The explanation of culture change: models in prehistory, (ed. C. Renfrew), 539-58.

Roe, F.E.S., 1966. "The Battle-Axe Series in Britain", Proceedings of the Prehistoric Society 32, 199-245.

Schultze-Motel, J., 1969. "Kulturpflanzenfunde der Becherkulturen" in Die neolitischen Becherkulturen im Gebiet der DDR und ihre europäischen Beziehungen (ed. H. Behrens & F. Schlette), 169-72.

Shennan, S., 1975. "The social organisation at Branc", Antiquity 49, 279-88.

Simpson, D.D.A., 1971. "Beaker houses and settlements in Britain", in Economy and Settlement in Neolithic and Early Bronze Age Britain and Europe, (ed. D.D.A. Simpson), 131-52.

Simpson, D.D.A., 1976. "The later Neolithic and Beaker settlement at Northton, Isle of Harris" in Settlement and Economy in the Third and Second Millennia B.C., ed. C. Burgess & R. Miket (British Archaeological Reports 33), 221-31.

Simpson, W.G., 1976. "A barrow cemetery of the second millennium B.C. at Tallington, Lincolnshire", Proceedings of the Prehistoric Society 42, 215-46.

Smith, A.G., 1975. "Neolithic and Bronze Age landscape changes in northern Ireland", in The effect of Man on the landscape: the Highland Zone (Research Report no 11, Council for British Archaeology), ed. Evans, J.G., Limbrey, S. and Cleere, H., 64-73.

Startin, D.W.A., 1976. Mathematics and Manpower (B. Phil Thesis, Oxford).

Taylor, J.J., 1970. "Lunulae Reconsidered", Proceedings of the Prehistoric Society 36, 38-81.

Thurnam, J., 1871. "On Ancient British Barrows, expecially those of Wiltshire and the adjoining Counties (Part II, Round Barrows)", Archaeologia 43, 285-522.

Ucko, P.J., 1969/70. "Ethnography and archaeological interpretation of funerary remains", World Archaeology 1, 262-80.

van Wijngaarden-Bakker, L.H., 1974. "The animal remains from the Beaker settlement at Newgrange, Co. Meath: First Report", Proceedings of the Royal Irish Academy 74, C, 313-83.

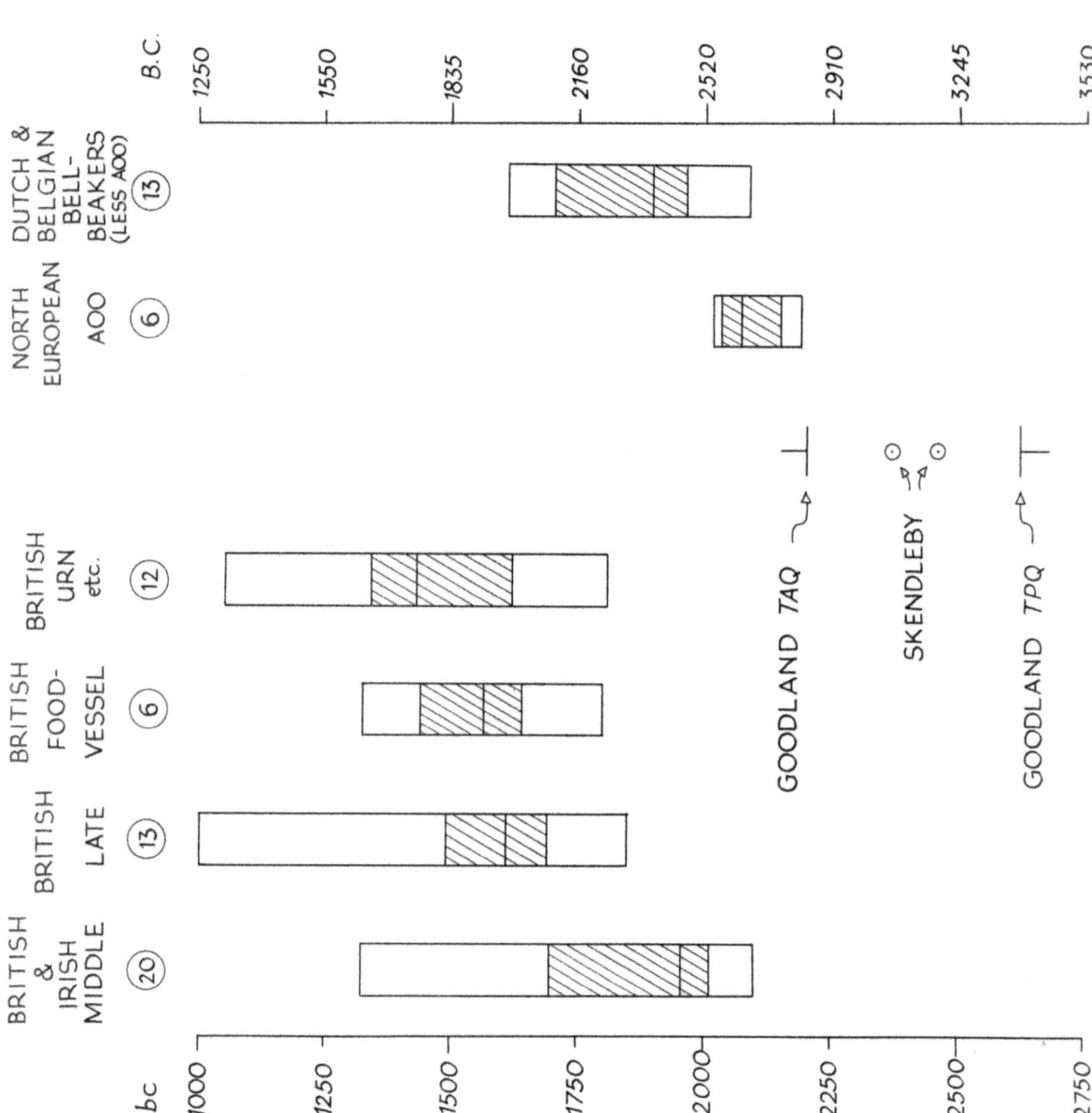

Fig. 4:1 Provisional dispersion-diagrams (after Ottaway 1973) of radiocarbon dates of material associated with: British and Irish Middle style beakers; British Late style beakers; Food Vessels and Urns; north European All-Over-Ornamented beakers; Dutch and Belgian bell-beakers (excluding All-Over-Ornamented but including Maritime beakers); also mean dates from Giants' Hills long barrow, Skendleby, and termini post and ante quem for the late phase at Goodland. Conventional radiocarbon time-scale (b c) to left, and calibrated (B.C.) to right after Clark (1975). The inner quartiles of the diagrams are hatched and the medians shown by a transverse line. Figures in circles indicate the number of dates from which each diagram has been constructed. The dates are those available to the author up to the end of February 1976.

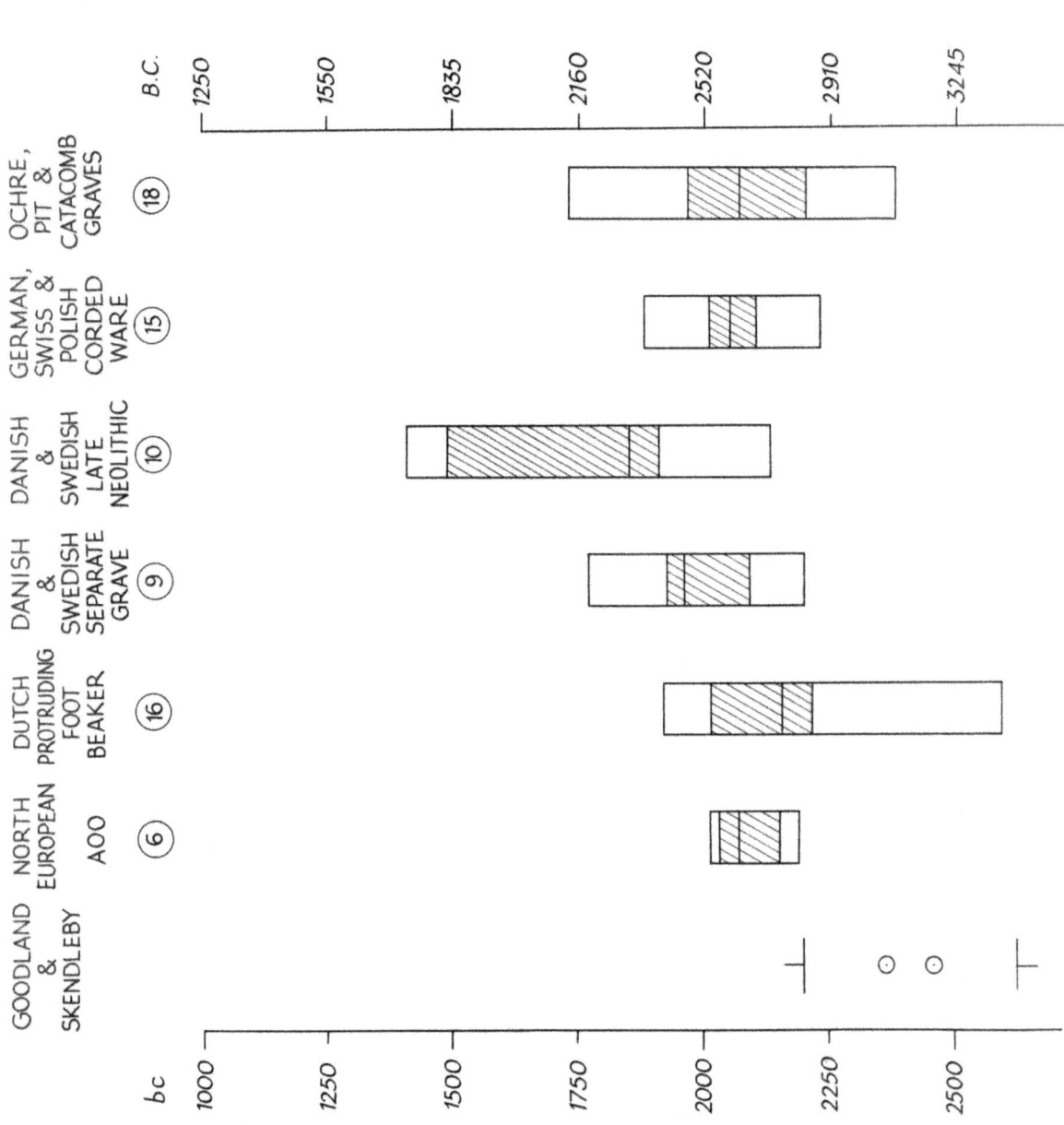

Fig. 4:2   Provisional dispersion-diagrams (after Ottaway 1973) of radiocarbon dates of material associated with: Goodland and Skendleby as on Fig. 1; north European All-Over-Ornamented beakers; Dutch Protuding Foot beakers; Danish and Swedish Separate Graves; Danish and Swedish Late Neolithic; German, Swiss and Polish Corded Ware graves or associations; Ochre, Pit and Catacomb Graves from eastern Europe and the Soviet Union. Conventional radiocarbon time-scale (b.c.) to left, and calibrated (B.C.) to right after Clark (1975). The inner quartiles of the diagrams are hatched and the medians shown by a transverse line. Figures in circles indicate the number of dates from which each diagram has been constructed. The dates are those available to the author up to the end of February 1976.

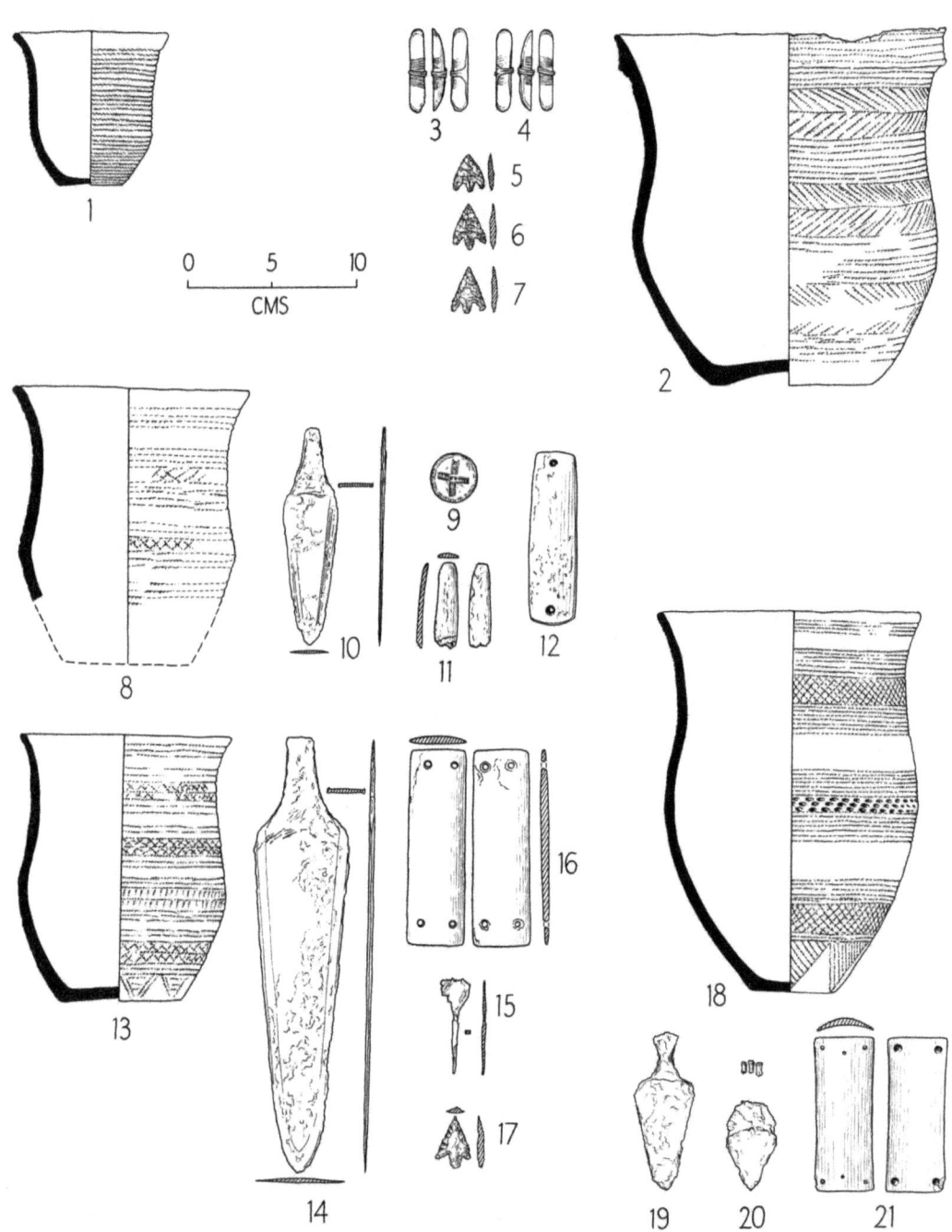

Fig. 4:3 Early style beaker: 1, Cassington, Oxon, ring-ditch 4. Gravegroups with Middle style beakers from southern England: 2-7, Radley, Oxon, barrow 4a; 8-12, Mere, Wilts, barrow G. 6a (12 after Colt Hoare); 13-17, Roundway, Wilts, barrow G. 8; 18-21, Dorchester, Oxon, Site XII (barrow). 1,2,8,13,18, beakers; 3,4,9, gold; 10,14,15,19, copper; 20, copper or bronze (one rivet, bronze); 12,16,21, slate; 5-7, 17, flint; 11, bone. 1-7, 18-21, Ashmolean; 8-11, 13-16, Devizes; 12, lost.

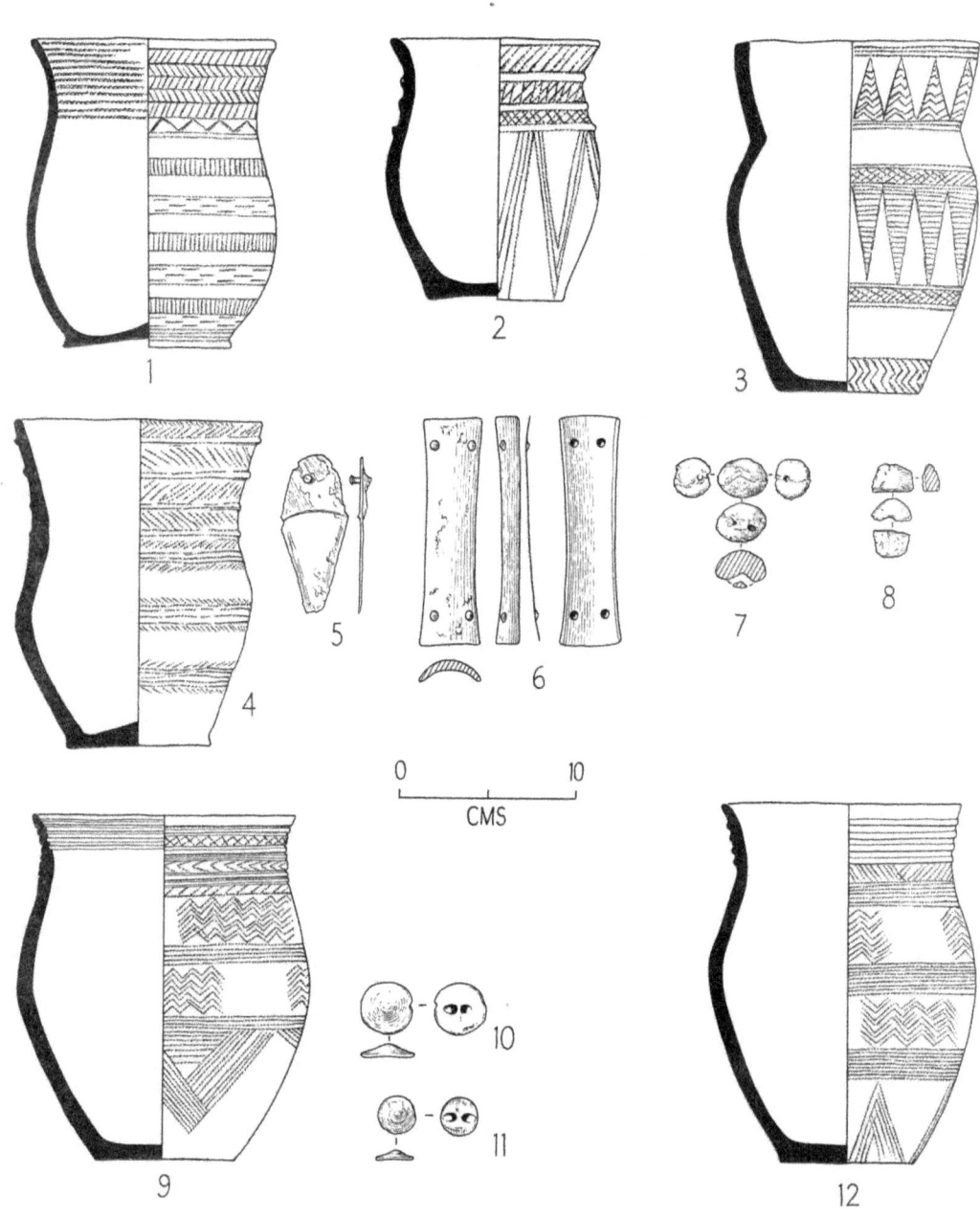

Fig. 4:4 Middle style beakers and grave-groups from northern England: 1-3, Goodmanham, East Riding, Yorks, barrow 99 (after Greenwell, Abercromby and Clarke); 4-8, Driffield, East Riding, Yorks, barrow; 9-12, Chatton Sandyford, Northumberland, barrow (after Jobey. 10 and 11 probably associated with 9). 1-4, 9,12, beakers; 5, copper or bronze; 6, slate with gold-capped copper or bronze studs; 7-8, amber; 10,11, jet. 1-8, British Museum; 9-12, Newcastle.

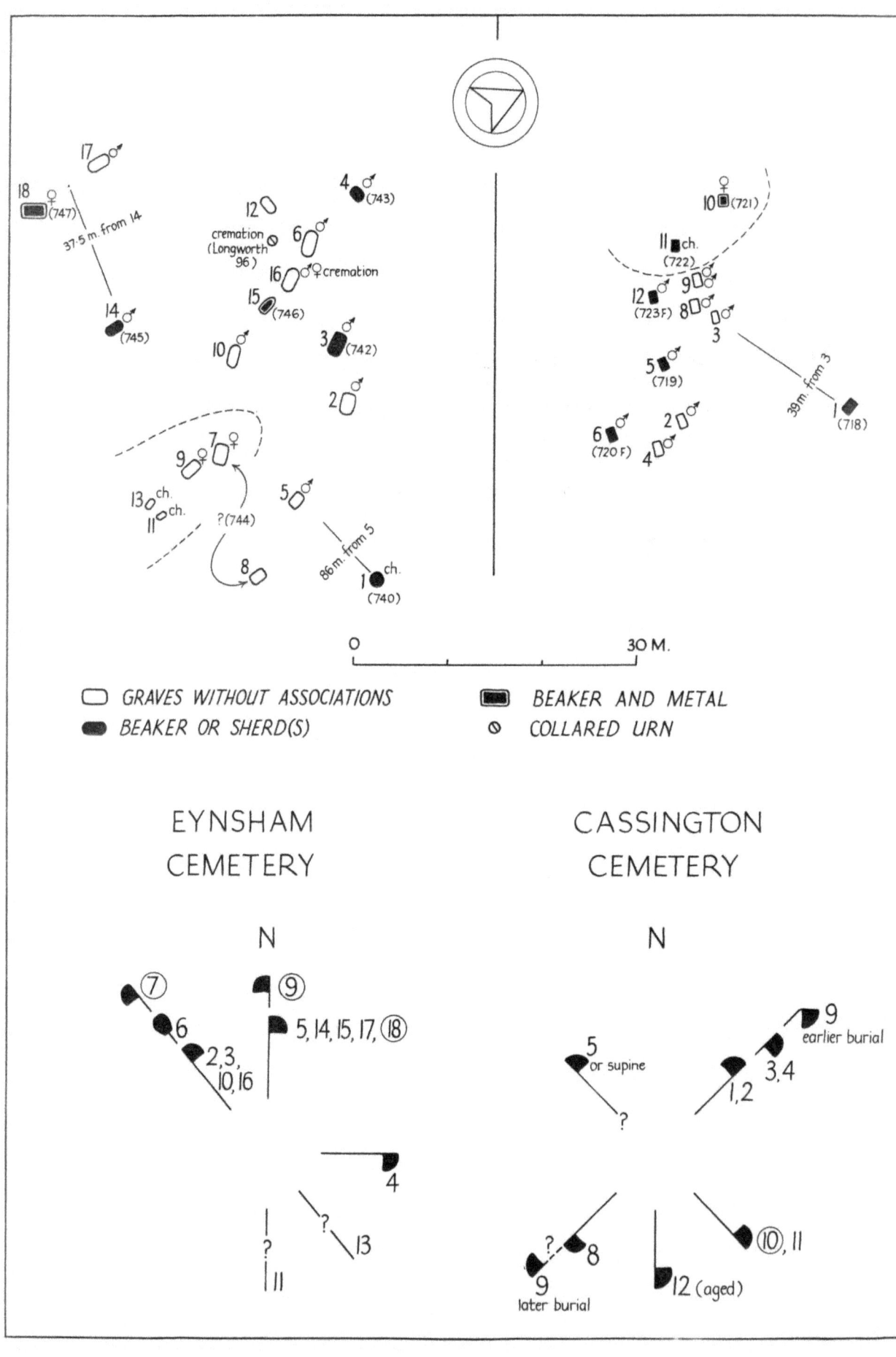

Fig. 4:5   Above: Diagram plans of Cassington (right) and Eynsham cemeteries (after Leeds and Musgrave), showing graves of men, women and children; beakers according to corpus numbers in Clarke(1970) and Collared Urn according to Longworth (1961).

Below: Diagram of orientations of skeletons in Cassington and Eynsham cemeteries (Thus for example, Eynsham 14 aligned north, facing east; Eynsham 2,6 and 7 aligned north-west, 2 facing north-east, 6 supine, 7 facing south-west). Women's graves in circles.

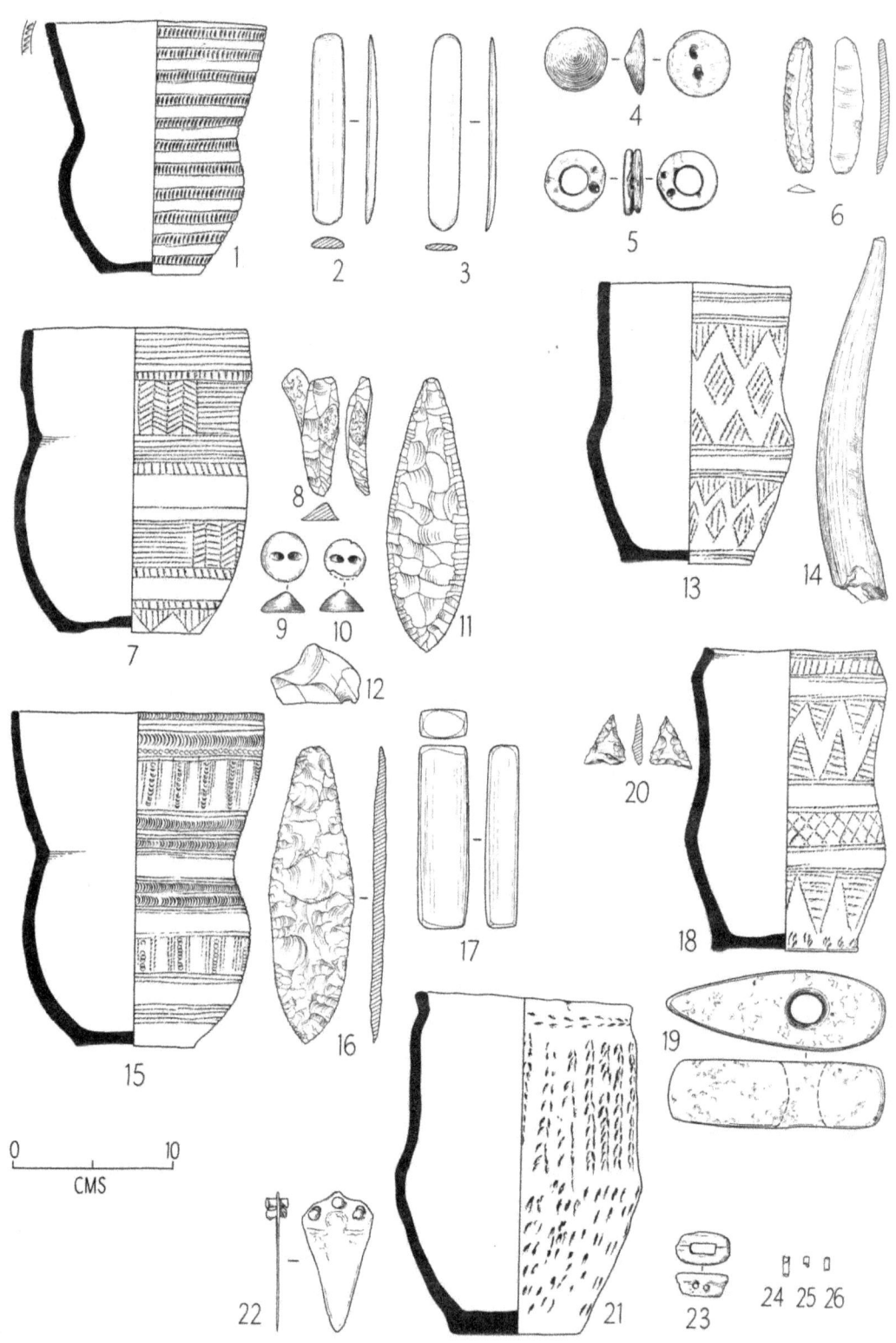

Fig. 4:6 Grave-groups with Late style beakers: 1-6, Winterbourne Stoke, Wilts, barrow G. 54; 7-11, Middleton-on-the-Wolds, East Riding, Yorks (after Hull Museum Publications, Abercromby and Clarke); 13-14, Brigmerston, Wilts, barrow; 15-17, Amesbury, Wilts, barrow G.4; 18-20, Durrington, Wilts, barrow G.67; 21-26, Eynsham, Oxon, cemetery grave 15. 1,7,13,15,18,21, beakers; 22, bronze (one rivet analysed); 24-6, copper or bronze; 2-3, slate; 17, ? siliceous hornstone; 19, tourmaline granite; 6,11,12,16,20, flint; 8, flint and iron ore; 4,5, shale; 9,10, jet; 23, bone; 14, antler. 1-6, 13-20, Devizes; 7-12, Hull; 21-6, Ashmolean.

www.ingramcontent.com/pod-product-compliance
Lightning Source LLC
Chambersburg PA
CBHW040949020526
44116CB00039B/2979